Schaumburg Township District Library

130 South Roselle Road

Schaumburg, Illinois 60193

BRAZIL
in Pictures

Tom Streissguth

⌐

Lerner Publications Company

918.1
STREISSGUTH,T

10/02
Lerner

Contents

Website address: www.lernerbooks.com

Lerner Publications Company
A division of Lerner Publishing Group
241 First Avenue North
Minneapolis, MN 55401 U.S.A.

web enhanced @ www.vgsbooks.com

CULTURAL LIFE 44

▶ Television. Music. Literature and Art. Religion. Holidays and Festivals. Sports. Food.

THE ECONOMY 56

▶ Industry. Agriculture. Energy and Mining. Foreign Trade. Transportation. Media and Communications. The Future.

FOR MORE INFORMATION

Library of Congress Cataloging-in-Publication Data

Streissguth, Thomas, 1958-
      Brazil in pictures / by Tom Streissguth.— Rev. and expanded.
         p.   cm. — (Visual geography series)
      Includes bibliographical references and index.
      Summary: An introduction to Brazil, discussing its history, government, economy, people, and culture.
      ISBN: 0-8225-1959-3 (lib. bdg. : alk. paper)
      1. Brazil. 2. Brazil—Pictorial works. [1. Brazil.] I. Title. II. Visual geography series (Minneapolis, Minn.)
F2508 .S74 2003
981—dc21   2001003275

Manufactured in the United States of America
1 2 3 4 5 6 - JR - 08 07 06 05 04 03

INTRODUCTION

In many ways, the Federative Republic of Brazil stands alone among the nations of Latin America. Although the kingdom of Spain explored and colonized the rest of Central and South America, Brazil was settled by the Portuguese. And although the Spanish colonies fought to become independent republics, Brazil established an empire after independence from Portugal. After peacefully proclaiming themselves a republic in 1889, the Brazilians saw immigrants arrive by the millions in their rapidly growing cities. Brazil was the largest and most populous nation of the region, drawing on its industry, agriculture, and mineral wealth to become an economic powerhouse—the fastest-growing nation, after post-World War II Japan, of the twentieth century.

The people of Brazil take great pride in their country's high rank in Latin America—first in resources, in size, in economic growth, even in the championship quality of their national soccer team. Modern Brazil also prides itself on being one of the world's most ethnically

diverse nations. The first Brazilians, the indigenous peoples of the Amazon River basin and the Atlantic coast, comprised two large languages groups but also divided themselves into hundreds of independent villages. The first Portuguese-speaking settlers were followed by a wave of European and Asian immigrants who began arriving in the late nineteenth century. Twenty-first-century Brazilians can trace their roots to Portugal, Italy, Spain, Germany, Great Britain, and Japan, as well as to indigenous peoples of South America and to Africans brought to South America by slave merchants. Although Brazil's official language remains Portuguese, its popular music and religions have borrowed elements from Europe, Africa, and the rest of South America. A rich indigenous mythology blends with a variety of cults and folk beliefs imported from Africa, yet 90 percent of Brazilians are members of the Catholic Church. Brazilian music, fashion, and food belong uniquely to Brazil but have been successfully exported to the rest of the world.

Unfortunately for Brazil's modern society, one of the most important contributions to this demographic and cultural complexity was the slave trade. The country's colonial economy was largely dependent on labor-intensive agriculture, and Brazil held to slavery until 1888—longer than any other nation in the Western Hemisphere. Slavery left Brazil with an unhealthy legacy: a wide gap between the "haves" and "have-nots," whose station in life mainly depended on their ethnic origins. Throughout the country, this social and economic gap continues to the present day. There is a huge disparity in the quality of life between rich and poor Brazilians, with poverty, crime, hunger, and unemployment affecting a large mass of people in the country's urban areas. Sprawling slums known as favelas encircle the cities of São Paulo and Rio de Janeiro and make up much of the urban landscape in the poorer northeast region of the country. From time to time, these circumstances have made Brazil a tumultuous place, where social unrest has clashed with oppression and dictatorship.

These social disparities have been recognized by modern Brazilians as the source of many of the country's troubles. Rich and poor Brazilians also share regret over squandered opportunities and wasted resources. Brazil's economy grew dramatically in the mid-twentieth century, and the nation held a commanding lead in Latin America in mineral and industrial production. Mismanagement and corruption, however, hindered the economy and ended the country's chance for long-lasting and wide-ranging prosperity. After a military dictatorship was overthrown in 1985, the civilian governments of the 1990s scrambled to pay off foreign debts and reduce government spending. Brazil's old currency, the cruzeiro, was destroyed by many years of inflation. A new currency known as the real was introduced in 1994, and the economic situation began to improve. But it was too late to stop a decades-long migration of poor rural people to urban areas, which suffered overcrowding, pollution, and crime as a result.

While recognizing their country's problems, the people of Brazil also benefit from a spirit of improvisation and adaptation that allows them to cope with their many challenges. This quality is summed up in the Portuguese word *jeito*, which refers to bending the rules, when necessary, to get along, get ahead, or just survive. With the jeito spirit, and the human and natural resources that remain within this immense country, Brazilians have reason for optimism.

THE LAND

The Federative Republic of Brazil covers 3,286,488 square miles (8,512,004 square kilometers) of northeastern South America. The fifth-largest nation in the world, Brazil is as large as Europe and slightly larger than the continental United States. It borders French Guiana, Suriname, Guyana, and Venezuela in the north, Colombia in the northwest, Peru and Bolivia in the west, and Paraguay, Argentina, and Uruguay in the southwest. To the east stretches a 4,600-mile-long (7,400-km) coastline along the Atlantic Ocean.

◖ Brazil's Regions

Brazil is made up of twenty-six states and the federal district of Brasília. The country can be divided into five principal regions. The states of Bahia, Sergipe, Alagoas, Pernambuco, Paraíba, Rio Grande do Norte, Ceará, Piauí, and Maranhão comprise the north-eastern region, which covers about 20 percent of Brazil's territory. As the first region of Brazil to be settled by Europeans, the northeast was

economically and politically the most important region of colonial
times. But the region lost importance when gold deposits were discovered in the state of Minas Gerais in the southeast, and the population
and industrial boom began around the cities of São Paulo and Rio de
Janeiro. The northeast now remains the poorest section of Brazil and
is plagued by periodic droughts that bake the dry, scrubby hinterlands
known as the *sertão* ("large desert" in Portuguese). A fertile strip of
land allows limited agriculture along the coast, which also attracts
tourists to its historic cities and fine beaches.

The central-western region includes Brasília, the national capital,
and the states of Goiás, Mato Grosso, and Mato Grosso do Sul. The
Brazilian Highlands, an elevated plain reaching altitudes of between
1,000 and 3,000 feet (300 and 1,000 meters), dominates the region. The
moderate climate here supports savannas (grasslands), scattered cacti
and scrub, and the *cerrado,* or subtropical forest, where few roads or
trails penetrated until the 1970s. North of Brasília, the highlands of

Brazil has the world's largest **herd of commercial cattle.** This gaucho, or cowboy, guides a small herd across a pasture.

the Serra Geral do Paraná rise above the surrounding plateau. The central-western region supports large cattle ranches as well as small farms burned out of the forest by settlers and squatters.

The southeastern region includes the states of São Paulo, Minas Gerais, Espírito Santo, and Rio de Janeiro. Relatively small in area (350,000 sq. mi.; 910,000 sq. km), the southeast makes up for its size with a growing population of about 53 million and its standing as the country's industrial heartland. The temperate climate allows the cultivation of cereal grains, vegetables, citrus fruits, and coffee, Brazil's single most important export for more than a century. Minas Gerais ("General Mines" in Portuguese) holds valuable mineral deposits and has been Brazil's gold-mining center since the seventeenth century.

Paraná, Santa Catarina, and Rio Grande do Sul states cover the southern region. The south is the only region of Brazil that experiences a temperate, four-season climate. Rio Grande do Sul, Brazil's southernmost state, is famous throughout Latin America for its cattle farms and its hardworking gauchos, or cowboys. The flat savannas make this region ideal for raising livestock. Small mountain ranges, including the Serra Geral from Paraná to Santa Catarina, break up the plains of the south. The Serra do Mar Mountains begin at the coast northeast of Curitiba, rising away from the narrow coastal plain.

The northern region of Roraíma, Amapá, Tocantins, Amazonas, Pará, Acre, and Rondônia states is also known as Amazonia, an area roughly corresponding to the basin of the Amazon River and claiming 42 percent of Brazil's land. Covered by the largest tropical rain forest in the world, Amazonia is also the most sparsely populated region of the country, with some of its isolated regions still unexplored by outsiders. Half of all animal species on earth live in Amazonia, as do about one-third of the globe's primates. In the northernmost part of the region lie the Guiana Highlands, a mountain area near the Venezuelan border.

Dense **rain forest** foliage competes for sunlight in Amazonia. Have a look at vgsbooks.com for a variety of links to additional photographs, to listen to animal sounds, and to find out more about the Amazon rain forest.

Slash-and-burn methods in Brazil's Amazon rain forest clear land for agriculture but also destroy habitat for many plant and animal species found nowhere else in the world.

The Amazon basin has not escaped modern environmental problems and serious deforestation. As Brazilian farmers move into the region, new roads are built and land is cleared by the "slash-and-burn" method, in which trees and underbrush are cut, burned, and cleared to make way for new pasture and cropland. During the 1980s, the clearing of land destroyed the Amazon rain forest at the rate of nearly 8,000 square miles (20,800 sq. km) a year, a rate that accelerated in the 1990s. Such deforestation leads to soil erosion, to the contamination of waterways by runoff, and to a loss of habitat for Brazilian wildlife. To help manage the forest, Brazil is constructing the Amazon Surveillance System (or SIVAM, from its initials in Portuguese). SIVAM will be a complex system of more than nine hundred computers throughout the Amazon rain forest, receiving information from satellites, radars, meteorological stations, high-altitude weather balloons, and various telecommunications media. The government intends to use SIVAM to detect illegal deforestation activities, fires, and drug smuggling and to protect indigenous communities.

⊙ Rivers

Brazil's navigable waterways run a total of 15,814 miles (25,445 km), divided among eight different river basins. Navigable waters, however, account for only part of the country's immense river system, which is dominated by the Amazon River. Fed by thousands of tributaries large and small, the Amazon follows a 3,990-mile (6,420-km) easterly course from its sources in the Andes Mountains of western South America. At its mouth, where 80 million gallons (300 million liters) of water flow into the Atlantic Ocean each second, the Amazon is about 90 miles (145 km) wide. For much of its length, one distant bank of this river is invisible from the other side.

The tide comes in, and the tide goes out—even at Manaus, more than 500 miles (800 km) upstream from the Atlantic Ocean. The spring tides of the Amazon River at Manaus can rise as high as 50 feet (15 m).

The Amazon was named by Spanish explorers of the sixteenth century, who imagined a great tribe of female warriors—the Amazons of ancient Greek mythology—lurking in the dark forests that rise at the river's edge. Certainly many unique species live within the Amazon rain forest. The world's largest rodent, the capybara, makes its home here, as do howler monkeys, anteaters, and several hundred species of snakes.

The howler monkey, which lives in Brazil's Amazon rain forest, is one of the largest monkeys in the Western Hemisphere. Its average head and body length is 22 to 36 inches (56 to 91 centimeters) and its tail measures 23 to 36 inches (52 to 91 cm) long.

As it flows through a flat and low-lying plain, the Amazon remains a wide and quiet waterway, with little turbulence and few dangerous rapids. Driftwood, sandbars, floating vegetation, and islands that cover the river's main channels in a series of long, verdant archipelagoes (groups of islands) hinder navigation. Along the riverbanks, indigenous groups and others who depend on the Amazon as a means of transportation and communication and as a source of food have built small villages.

The Paraná River (2,485 mi. long; 4,000 km) flows south through the Pantanal region and forms a portion of Brazil's border with Paraguay. Brazil meets the borders of Paraguay and Argentina near the Iguaçu Falls, a long series of towering waterfalls that stretches for miles along a crescent-shaped basin. The Pantanal itself is a huge, swampy ecological preserve about half the size of Texas. A single road, known as the Transpantaneira, leads visitors through the largest freshwater wetland on earth, which is home to river otters, jaguars, macaws, and more than six hundred varieties of birds and eighty mammal species found nowhere else on earth. In recent years, the flora and fauna of the Pantanal have been threatened by cattle ranchers who are clearing land for their livestock herds and by hydroelectric projects on the western edge of the region that are draining many of the rivers and streams vital

As **the broad, winding Amazon River** meanders across Brazil, sandbars and islands impede travel.

Scarlet macaws are one of more than six hundred species of birds inhabiting the region along the Brazil-Paraguay border.

to the survival of endangered fish, birds, reptiles, and mammals.

The São Francisco River flows 1,800 miles (2,896 km) through northeastern Brazil. It brings water and waterpower to the dry, hot country. The São Francisco empties into the Atlantic Ocean north of the small port of Aracaju. A dam on the São Francisco at Paulo Afonso provides hydroelectric power to the state of Bahia and the cities of the coast.

Climate

Most of Brazil lies within the tropics, yet the climate varies widely with elevation, distance from the sea, and distance from the equator, which runs just north of and roughly parallel to the Amazon River. Most of Brazil lies south of the equator, where winter occurs in the middle of the calendar year and summer begins in December.

Year-round humidity and heavy seasonal rains characterize the north, the only purely tropical region of the country. Central Brazil has hot summers and cooler, drier winters. The southern states enjoy temperate climates, with occasional freezing temperatures and winter snowfalls in the high elevations.

The highest average temperatures occur in the interior parts of the dry northeast, which averages 79° to 82°F (26° to 28°C) year-round. The southern region and higher elevations of the southeast feel the coldest, with a mean annual temperature of 64°F (18°C). The heaviest rainfall in Brazil is in the coastal highlands of the Serra do Mar and in western Amazonia, a region that can get more than 140 inches (356 cm) of rain a year. The driest areas of the northeast receive less than 20 inches (51 cm) annually and much less during periods of drought.

Natural Resources

The first European explorers came to South America in search of valuable trade goods and natural resources. Over the centuries, prospectors and entrepreneurs made the most of these resources and carried out a busy foreign trade in timber, minerals, and spices. The land still holds rich deposits of gold, silver, lead, copper, nickel, tin, aluminum, zinc, phosphate, iron, and titanium. Brazil has the world's largest deposits of manganese ore. Precious and semiprecious stones including diamonds, amethysts, topaz, rock crystal, and aquamarine have also been unearthed. The southern states of Rio Grande do Sul and Santa Catarina produce coal, which has also been discovered in limited quantities in the Amazon basin. Minas Gerais state, Brazil's mineral treasure-house, boasts large reserves of iron ore.

Brazil is also home to the third-largest reserve of timber in the world. A forest covering about one million square miles (2,590,000 sq. km) encircles the Amazon basin and includes more than four hundred different species of hardwood trees. Mahogany, brazilwood, and jacaranda trees are the principal commercially valuable species.

For energy production, the most valuable natural resource has been the country's large store of fresh water. The enormous Amazon basin, which covers about 60 percent of Brazil's territory, includes 20 percent of all the fresh water on earth. Rivers provide the basic fuel for hydropower plants, which have made the country a self-sufficient electricity producer.

Cities

Brazil's urban population makes up nearly 80 percent of its total population, one of the highest such percentages in the world. The country's post-World War II industrialization brought large-scale migration into cities that promised better wages and a higher standard of living for rural families, many of whom were only a generation or two removed from plantation slavery. As the twenty-first century began, however, Brazil's large cities had lost much of their original appeal. Traffic congestion, crime, and pollution have all taken their toll on Rio de Janeiro, São Paulo, and other urban concentrations. Many young Brazilians are moving out of the large cities and into sub-urban and exurban areas, where the quality of life is better.

SÃO PAULO With a population of 10.4 million, São Paulo is the largest city of South America and the third-largest city on earth—only Mexico City and Tokyo are larger. A national financial center, São Paulo and its surrounding state have also become an industrial powerhouse, making up one-half of the Brazilian economy. Major European, North American, and Asian banks have important branches in downtown São Paulo, which also forms the seat of the Bolsa de Valores do São Paulo, or Bovespa, Latin America's busiest stock exchange.

Founded in 1554, São Paulo remained a small and poor settlement until the discovery of gold in the mountains of what is now Minas Gerais. A ramshackle but busy frontier city, it grew into an international business center under the Brazilian Empire, the state that declared its independence from Portugal in the early nine-teenth century. As the surrounding region flourished from mining as well as coffee production and export, the city attracted foreign investment from Europe, giving rise to a class of wealthy entrepre-neurs that has wielded most of Brazil's economic and political power ever since.

The **business district of São Paulo** generates much of the economic activity in Brazil. For a link to the most up-to-date population figures for Brazil, go to vgsbooks.com.

VENEZUELA

COLOMBIA

GUYANA

SURINAME

FRENCH
GUIANA

ATLANTIC
OCEAN

ECUADOR

GUIANA HIGHLANDS

Jari River

MARAJÓ
ISLAND

Equator

Amazon River

Rio Negro

Amazon River

Pará River

NORTHERN

AMAZON BASIN

NORTHEASTERN

Sertão

PERU

BRAZILIAN

CENTRAL
WESTERN

SERRA GERAL
DO PARANÁ

São Francisco River

BOLIVIA

Paraguay River

PANTANAL

HIGHLANDS

SOUTHEASTERN

Pico da Bandeira ▲

River

CHILE

PACIFIC OCEAN

PARAGUAY

Paraná

Iguaçu Falls

SERRA DO MAR

Guanabara Bay

SOUTHERN

ARGENTINA

URUGUAY

Brazil

Feet	Meters	
9843	3000	Mountains
6582	2000	Uplands
3281	1000	
1640	500	Lowlands

Elevation

N

—— International border
▲ Mountain peak

ATLANTIC
OCEAN

0   500 Miles
0   500 KM

Slum housing and rubbish heaps contrast sharply with the modern skyscrapers that dominate São Paulo's skyline.

São Paulo also benefited from the country's rapid economic growth in the middle of the twentieth century. By the 1970s, a towering forest of skyscrapers was rising in the center of the city, where streets continue to be jammed with pedestrians and slow-moving cars, buses, and taxis. But São Paulo also contains vast and poverty-ridden favelas, or slums, and more than three million people live in the overcrowded tenement buildings known as *cortiços.* These slums and the desperation of the poor have bred crime, prostitution, violence, and drug trafficking, problems that touch many of the young and the poor.

Attracted by jobs and housing availability in a rapidly growing city, Japanese immigrants played an important role in the growth of São Paulo as a business and industrial center. At the end of the 1990s, São Paulo was home to the second largest Japanese community outside of Japan. The largest such community lives in the state of Hawaii.

RIO DE JANEIRO The former capital of Brazil, Rio de Janeiro (population 5.8 million), is famous around the world for its dramatic physical setting. Along the western entry to Guanabara Bay, office buildings, apartments, and monuments tumble across several narrow plains. The jumble extends to the bay and the Atlantic Ocean along a series of long, curving beaches. Steep ridges break the city into a checkerboard of compact, crowded urban clusters, connected by underground tunnels and a modern subway system.

Rio de Janeiro was founded by the Portuguese captain Estácio de Sá, who arrived with a fleet near the towering Sugarloaf Mountain on March 1, 1565. Rio replaced Salvador as Brazil's capital in 1763, and from 1815 until 1821 it was the royal capital of the Portuguese empire. Its status as an imperial capital attracted talented European artists, architects, and writers. Its importance as a spiritual center is symbolized by a 98-foot (29.4-m) figure of Christ the Redeemer, with arms outstretched, that rises on the Corcovado (Hunchback) peak overlooking Guanabara Bay.

The inhabitants of Rio de Janeiro, known by the nickname *cariocas*, enjoy a reputation as easygoing and fun-loving, in contrast to the serious and businesslike character Brazilians associate with the *paulistas*, residents of São Paulo. Rio offers lively nightlife and cultural attractions and has become South America's most popular tourist destination. But the city also suffers one of the highest urban crime rates in the world, a rate that in some years has included more than ten thousand homicides. Although kidnappings, bank robberies, and auto theft have plagued the city, most of the crime in Rio de Janeiro is caused by the selling and buying of illegal drugs, an activity that employs a large population of young people from the city's poor hillside favelas.

Cristo Redentor, or Christ the Redeemer, overlooking **Rio de Janeiro,** was commissioned for the one-hundredth anniversary of Brazil's independence from Portugal in 1822.

BRASÍLIA Proclaimed as the "city of the future," the national capital of Brasília was officially inaugurated on April 21, 1960. Largely the brain-child of President Juscelino Kubitschek, who was determined to make a futuristic nation out of Brazil, the city was designed by Lucio Costa and Oscar Niemeyer to represent the nation's progress and leadership in Latin America. However, the capital cost more than $10 billion to design and build, a price that staggered the public treasury. The heavy costs contributed to steep inflation that lasted for three decades and played havoc with the Brazilian economy.

By the year 2001, Brasília had reached a population of about two million, many of whom lived in distant "satellite cities" far from the capital's main avenues. Although it has avoided the common urban problems of pollution, congestion, and crime, central Brasília has also turned out to be mainly a home of government bureaucrats and politicians—a place where empty sidewalks create an air of sterility and isolation.

SECONDARY CITIES The largest city and capital of Amazonas state, Manaus (population 1.2 million) was founded during a short-lived rubber boom of the nineteenth and early twentieth centuries. The rubber plantations of the surrounding forests fed an insatiable worldwide demand for automobile tires, a business that made a few local planters wealthy enough to decorate their homes and their city with the finest imported goods and materials from Europe. The population of Manaus exploded to more than one million before the rubber market collapsed in 1913.

The city of Belo Horizonte (population 2.2 million), the capital of Minas Gerais, was the center of the mining boom that began in the eighteenth century. The gold rush also saw the rise of Ouro Prêto, founded in 1698, which has managed to preserve much of its original architecture, civic monuments, and churches along its colonial-era streets. Salvador (population 2.4 million), the capital of Bahia, was the original colonial capital of Brazil. African culture, brought by the captive slaves that arrived in the port during three centuries of legal slavery, survives in the clothing, speech dialects, and religious practices of many residents. Annual summer festivals, which begin in early December, celebrate this Afro-Brazilian heritage with music, dance, and religious observances.

HISTORY AND GOVERNMENT

Archaeologists working in the Amazon basin have discovered the remains of humans who lived in this region as early as twelve thousand years ago, and new studies suggest that the first Brazilians may have lived here as early as forty thousand years ago. The indigenous peoples were divided into hundreds of tribes that fell into four major language groups—the Tupi-Guarani, Gê, Carib, and Arawak. The Tupi-Guarani were the largest and most aggressive group, often engaging other tribes in warfare.

▶ Europeans Arrive

By the fifteenth century, Europeans were searching for a faster and safer route to eastern Asia, where European merchants had traded silk, spices, and other valuable goods for centuries. The land route had become risky and expensive, as much of the route was conquered by states hostile to Europe. Captains from Spain, Italy, and Portugal began exploring the unknown seas to the west.

The Portuguese were well prepared for this age of exploration. They inhabited a poor and isolated region of the Iberian Peninsula in south-western Europe, but they also possessed a convenient jumping-off point for sea voyages to Africa and the Indian Ocean. Portugal's kings sponsored many voyages of exploration, knowing that overseas colonies would help their resource-poor nation. In 1441 Portuguese shipyards began producing the caravel, a swift vessel that was ideal for the navigation of seacoasts and large rivers. Prince Henry the Navigator, the son of King João I, established a school of navigation at Sagres, the southwestern tip of the European continent.

Under Henry's direction, Portugal's fleets explored and colonized several island chains in the Atlantic Ocean, including the Azores, Madeira, the Cape Verde Islands, and São Tomé. In 1497 Vasco da Gama discovered a route to Asia around the Cape of Good Hope, at the southern tip of Africa. Da Gama was followed by Pedro Álvars Cabral, who set out from Lisbon, Portugal's capital, on March 9, 1500. To avoid storms, Cabral's fleet of thirteen ships set a westerly course, and in April sighted the eastern coast of South America. Anchoring in what is now Pôrto Seguro, Cabral named the new land Terra da Vera Cruz, or Land of the True Cross.

Cabral claimed the land for the king of Portugal. By the Treaty of Tordesillas, which had been signed in 1494, Portugal and Spain had agreed to divide new lands discovered by their explorers in the Americas. A line running north and south, fixed at 370 leagues (about 1,300 mi.; 2,000 km) west of the Cape Verde Islands, would mark the division. While Spain had the right to lands west of the Tordesillas line, Portugal claimed lands to the east—which included Pôrto Seguro and its hinterlands.

While several more expeditions followed Cabral to South America, Portuguese traders began dealing with the indigenous tribes along the coast. The hoped-for gold was, as yet, nowhere to be found. But the forests of Terra da Vera Cruz did provide colorful macaws, parrots, and other exotic birds, as well as the pith of the brazilwood tree, which furnished a valuable red dye. From this resource, exported from settlements around Recife in the northeast, the Portuguese gave their colony its permanent name: Brazil.

On their own, traders could do little to enrich the Portuguese treasury. Profiting from the resources of Brazil required permanent settlements and colonists, who began arriving with the expedition of Martim Afonso de Sousa. De Sousa established a colony at São Vicente in 1532. With the goal of attracting wealthy colonial governors to the hard task of developing the new land, the king of Portugal divided Brazil into fifteen territories known as captaincies. Each captaincy came under the control of a donatory, a Portuguese citizen with close ties to the king. While the ownership of the colony remained with the crown, the donatories had the right to govern their captaincies and administer justice as they saw fit. They also made grants of land known as *sesmarias* to individual farmers.

A steady stream of colonists arrived from Portugal throughout the sixteenth and seventeenth centuries. Many were poor farmers or artisans who had little opportunity in their home country. Others were exiles or prisoners, known in Portuguese as *degredados.* Eventually, the intermarriage of Portuguese colonists with indigenous peoples led to a new social class in Brazil, known as *mamelucos* or *caboclos.*

An indigenous audience watches Cabral and his crew attend their first Mass onshore in Brazil.

FIVE-HUNDREDTH ANNIVERSARY

The year 2000 marked the five-hundredth anniversary of the so-called discovery of Brazil by the Portuguese. Many Brazilians refused to embrace official celebrations—especially Brazil's indigenous peoples. Their spokespeople publicly criticized official events. They called these celebrations insensitive to the native population. Indigenous and Afro-Brazilian organizations, as well as others, spearheaded a counter event, called Brazil, The Other 500. Its purpose was to raise awareness about the five hundred years of massacres, invasions, slavery, and neglect inflicted on the native population and to promote discussion about Brazil's rich cultural diversity.

The colonists had little regard for the cultural and linguistic differences among tribal groups. They generally treated all indigenous people like children, in need of discipline and conversion to Catholicism. Many native villages moved inland, into the plains and forests that lay, for a time, out of reach of European settlers. Many of those who remained behind were enslaved by the Europeans or died of European diseases to which they had no immunity.

By the end of the sixteenth century, the cultivation and refining of sugarcane had become the principal business of Brazil. Where they found the proper soil and climate conditions, the Brazilians also raised tobacco, a cash crop much in demand in Europe. Spices were grown and harvested, and as a staple crop, Brazil's farmers raised manioc, a root plant native to the Americas that was eaten like potatoes or made into flour.

As did other European colonizers, the Portuguese saw their American colony as a source of trade goods and raw materials that could be sold on the European market. As the colony grew, Brazil came to provide an important market for finished goods manufactured in Portugal. There was more to colonization than money and trade goods, however. The Roman Catholic Church, the dominant church of Portugal and Spain, considered the conversion of native Americans one of its most important endeavors. For this reason, the king allowed the Jesuits, the Franciscans, and other Christian brotherhoods to undertake the mission of converting indigenous Brazilians to Christianity. The priests gathered their charges into permanent villages, where they also tried to convert them from the hunting and gathering life to settled agriculture. Brazil's first episcopate, or religious seat, was founded in 1552 in the colonial capital of Salvador.

Slavery in Brazil

Although sugar was Brazil's main export, Brazilian landowners faced a lack of willing laborers for the hard and dangerous task of cultivating cane. Attempts to force indigenous groups into bondage failed, as most of the native South Americans could not adapt to heavy agricultural work. To meet their need for labor, Brazilian landowners turned to the market in African slaves, provided by English and Dutch merchants who carried on a three-way trade among Africa, Brazil, and Europe. From posts along the west coast of Africa, these merchants transported Africans to Salvador and Rio de Janeiro, the principal slave ports of Brazil. At slave markets, Brazil's landowners paid in silver or in tobacco, an important medium of exchange in the New World colonies.

Brazil imported more slaves than any other nation in the Western Hemisphere. Among Brazilian colonists, it was a mark of prestige and status to own slaves, and people of all economic and social classes took part in the trade. But slave escapes and rebellions brought frequent turmoil to the colony's plantations. Escaped slaves formed their own semi-independent states, known as *quilombos*, in the vast interior. The largest of these, Palmares, covered 17,000 square miles (44,030 sq. km) in a series of remote valleys, more than twenty days' march from the coast. Palmares welcomed not only escaped African slaves but also indigenous, European, and mixed-race refugees, all of whom obeyed only the state's leader, King Zumbí, and defended themselves with strong log walls, deadly forest mantraps, and guerrilla warfare. Palmares resisted several attacks from Brazil's rulers until 1695, when a Portuguese army overran its hilltop palisade walls, prompting King Zumbí and more than two hundred of his followers to commit suicide.

Cultivation and refinement of sugarcane was the principal business in Brazil by the end of the sixteenth century.

Slavery became an integral part of colonial agriculture, which in turn played a vital role in the European economy. In 1649, to extend further control over the transatlantic trade, King Dom João IV of Portugal formed the Brazil Company. The company operated a fleet of thirty-six ships that served as escorts for merchants transporting their goods to and from Brazil. Armed with muskets and cannons, these ships discouraged attack by rival navies and by the privateers who infested the Caribbean and the coastal waters of South America. The Brazil Company held a monopoly on the trade in manioc flour, wine, and cod between Brazil and Portugal.

In the meantime, land explorers known as *bandeirantes* pushed into the interior in search of cultivable land, precious metals, and slaves collected from the indigenous tribes. The discovery of gold in Minas Gerais in 1695 led to a population boom and to a gradual southward movement of settlers. Gold from Brazil was transported directly to workshops in Portugal and eventually found its way into the king's treasury.

> Soon after gold was discovered in the Minas Gerais region, a civil war broke out. Newly arrived prospectors from Rio de Janeiro battled local bandeirantes, who considered the land and its resources as their property. In Brazilian history this conflict is known as the Guerra dos Emboabas, or War of the Dressed Legs. The name came from a disparaging phrase, used by many indigenous people for the Portuguese, that compared the colorful stockings of the Europeans to birds with feathers on their legs.

In 1727 Brazil gained another valuable export with the arrival of the first coffee plant, brought to Brazil from French Guiana. Coffee flourished in the climate and soil along the Paraíba River of the southeast as well as in the state of Paraná. In the meantime, settlement of Brazil was moving past these new plantations and as far south as a trade route known as the River Plate, where the Brazilian colonists were stopped at the Spanish settlements of what is now Uruguay. These trends benefited Rio de Janeiro, where the trade in timber, sugar, gold, and slaves transformed this small port into the busiest town in the colony, eventually surpassing the old capital of Salvador. In 1763 Rio de Janeiro became the capital of Brazil.

By the Treaty of Madrid in 1750, Spain and Portugal settled their boundary disputes in Brazil. Four years later, the Brazilian captaincies

PROFESSIONAL BANDITS

The resource-rich São Francisco Valley saw its share of violence during Brazil's colonial history. Armies of professional bandits known as *capangas* roamed the region, hiring themselves out to plantation owners, local city governments, feuding clans, and mining companies. The landscape of deep gulleys and thick forest allowed for deadly ambushes, and there were plenty of natural resources available for the needed supplies: saltpeter for gunpowder, silver ore for bullets, and iron for swords and lances.

were abolished. The Portuguese crown took direct control of the colony, which it ruled through a royal governor.

The authoritarian rule sparked discontent among poor farmers and town dwellers. Revolutions in the United States and France in the late 1700s gave

The hills of Ouro Prêto in the São Francisco Valley *(above left)* were once densely forested. They provided good cover for colonial-era bandits.

inspiration for Brazilians seeking an end to monarchy and the establishment of a republic. A series of independence movements sprang up in defiance of Portuguese control, especially in the northeastern regions. The strongest of these was led by Joaquim José da Silva Xavier, whose occupation as a dentist earned him the nickname Tiradentes (the Tooth-puller). An opponent of slavery, Tiradentes saw the Portuguese monarchy as a decrepit and corrupt institution that was preventing Brazil from realizing its enormous potential as a democratic republic. Tiradentes gathered thousands of followers and defied royal authority until 1789, when he was captured and publicly executed.

Independence

In the late 1790s, a young French officer, Napoleon Bonaparte, rose to power at the head of the French army. During the next few years, Napoleon campaigned across Europe, defeating rival armies, overthrowing kings, and establishing new republics. His drive into the Iberian Peninsula in 1808 forced the young regent of Portugal, João, to flee the country with fifteen thousand of his courtiers, officials, and subjects. The royal fleet arrived in Brazil, where the regent established his new court in Rio de Janeiro. In 1816, a year after Napoleon's final defeat, João was crowned king of Portugal as João VI. Instead of returning to Europe, however, João's court remained in Brazil, an act of defiance that lent great prestige to the colony. Many Portuguese began to consider Brazil the future seat of the Portuguese empire.

In the meantime, Napoleon had been banished from Europe. In the wake of the Napoleonic Wars, Europe's diplomats redrew the borders of their continent and returned exiled monarchs to their thrones. After his

Fleeing to Brazil to escape an advancing army led by **Napoleon Bonaparte** *(left)*, João, the future king of Portugal, was crowned in Rio de Janeiro.

rule was officially restored in Portugal, King João returned in 1821, leaving behind his son and heir, Dom Pedro, to rule Brazil.

A strong movement for independence continued in Brazil, and Dom Pedro became exasperated with the Portuguese government, which demanded that he capture and punish Brazil's defiant rebels. In 1822, at the Ypiranga River, Dom Pedro gathered a procession of followers and proclaimed "Independência ou morte!"— "Independence or death!" The famous "Cry of Ypiranga" established Brazil as its own empire, under the leadership of Dom Pedro as Emperor Pedro I. The only violence occurred in the state of Bahia, where Portuguese troops resisted but were driven out. In 1824 Brazil ratified its first constitution, modeled in large part on the Constitution of the United States. In the next year, Portugal recognized the independence of its former colony.

Dom Pedro had gained Brazil's independence, but he ruled the country with little regard for the new legislature set up by the nation's constitution. Social unrest roiled the empire, while the defiance of plantation owners and the military weakened the monarch's authority. In 1831 Dom Pedro abdicated (gave up) his crown, an act that left his five-year-old son as the new regent. In 1840 the son succeeded his father as Emperor Dom Pedro II.

The rule of Dom Pedro II brought important progress to Brazil. Coffee replaced sugar as the nation's most important export, a position it would hold until 1973. New cities were established in the interior, where roads and rail links improved communications. Large plantations in the Amazon forests were cleared to meet the rising demand for rubber in North America and Europe.

Brazil also fought several small wars to establish its final boundaries with Argentina, Paraguay, and Uruguay. The most important of these was the War of the Triple Alliance, begun in 1865, in which Brazil joined Argentina and Uruguay to fight the landlocked nation of Paraguay. The end of the war came in 1870, when Brazilian troops surrounded and killed Francisco Solano López, the Paraguayan president.

◉ The Republic

More than any other nation in the Western Hemisphere, Brazil still depended on slave labor. Slavery had been abolished in the British colonies even before Brazilian independence, and the U.S. Civil War had ended slavery in the United States in 1865. As a result, the business of slave trading came to an end, while rural labor was provided by a growing number of immigrants from Europe. Diplomatic and economic pressure from abroad finally convinced Dom Pedro II to

Emperor Dom Pedro II, the second ruler of independent Brazil, was a well-liked monarch.

banish slavery by law in 1888. Although the institution of slavery had ended, it left a legacy of social division and economic discrimination that continues in modern Brazil.

Pedro II was a popular monarch throughout most of his reign, but the emancipation of the slaves caused great discontent among Brazil's powerful landowners, who saw their economic interests and way of life threatened by the loss of their slaves. Also, army officers resented Pedro II for cutting the military budget after the War of the Triple Alliance. Many Brazilians were frustrated by the monarchy and demanded that Brazil become a republic. In November 1889, civilians and military officers hatched a conspiracy to overthrow the monarchy. Rather than fight the conspiracy, Dom Pedro II abdicated his position, and a new Brazilian republic was founded. A new constitution, ratified in 1891, established the elective office of the president of the republic. Brazil still did not enjoy full democracy, however, as the first president, General Manuel Deodoro da Fonseca, ruled his country by decree.

The dictatorship of Fonseca and his successors led groups within the military to splinter and fight for power. In 1894 the military yielded power to the republic's first civilian ruler, President Prudente José de Morais Barros. During the next sixteen years, Brazil enjoyed an orderly succession of elected presidents. New industries were established in the cities while rural landowners profited from the export of tobacco, rubber, and coffee.

Another military officer, Hermes Rodrigues da Fonseca (a nephew of Manuel de Fonseca) was elected president in 1910. Opposition to his dictatorial rule threw the country into turmoil, a situation worsened by the outbreak of World War I in Europe in 1914. Brazil joined the Allies in their fight against Germany and sent troops to Europe in 1917. High demand for rubber and other products helped the country's economy to recover, but after the war's end in 1918, coffee prices fell sharply, while a new process for making artificial rubber hurt one of Brazil's most important exports.

▶ Getulio Vargas

Through the 1920s, leaders from Minas Gerais and São Paulo shared the presidency of Brazil. In 1930 this arrangement came to a bitter end. Although a paulista (São Paulo) candidate, Júlio Prestes, won the election, the candidacy of rancher Getulio Vargas was supported by the military. Vargas succeeded to the presidency while the military prevented Prestes from taking office.

Vargas, the governor of Rio Grande do Sul, had also served in both state and federal governments as a legislator. An energetic, determined president, he attacked Brazil's social ills by introducing compulsory public education and a national health program. The government built new highways and railroads, and reclamation programs created productive farms and plantations. Under the slogan "Estado Nôvo" (New State), Vargas also invested public funds in the expansion of basic industries and the development of a new national identity.

Declaring that "Brazil is one huge hospital!" Getulio Vargas set out to improve health and nutrition among the Brazilians in the 1930s. Free clinics were established, and each company employing more than five hundred people was required to provide a meal at cost to its employees. The new workers' restaurants were meant to improve the Brazilians' ordinary starchy diet of rice, bread, and manioc. While dining on high-calorie meals of soup, beans, meat, vegetables, milk, cheese, and fruit, the patrons were treated to news, information, and health advice delivered via megaphone by an announcer.

A new constitution in 1934 granted important concessions to Brazilian workers and extended the right to vote to women. The Vargas government also founded state-owned oil and steel companies, laying the foundation for the country's rapid industrial growth in the following decades.

Under the Vargas presidency, Brazilians began to feel a growing sense of national unity and purpose. But Vargas and his supporters were unwilling to share power and unwilling to abide by the constitutional provision that a president could not serve consecutive terms. In 1937 Vargas called off a scheduled election, abolished rival political parties, and began strict censorship of the Brazilian media. A new constitution of that year also allowed the president to rule by decree, without the consent of the legislature.

In Europe, dictatorships were also flourishing in Italy and Spain, while Adolf Hitler, Germany's leader and head of the Nazi party, was vowing revenge for his country's defeat in World War I. Hitler carried out his threat by invading Poland in 1939, an event that touched off World War II. Brazil declared war on Germany in the summer of 1942. The Brazilian navy prevented German U-boats (submarines) from controlling the South Atlantic Ocean, and for the second time, Brazil became the only South American country to send troops overseas to fight in Europe.

At the war's end, Vargas came under harsh criticism from the public and from military leaders, who resented the tight control exercised over them by the central government. In October 1945, the army forced the president to

Brazilian soldiers salute **President Getulio Vargas,** *(center front)* as he carries out an inspection aboard a coast guard ship carrying soldiers to Europe to fight in World War II.

leave the capital and replaced him with Eurico Gaspar Dutra. A new constitution of 1946 again provided that no president could serve consecutive terms, a measure intended to prevent future dictatorships. Vargas remained popular in Brazil, however, and returned to the presidency by an open election in 1950.

Economic problems plagued Vargas's presidency, and he also suffered a public scandal over the attempted killing of a political enemy, Carlos Lacerda. The gunman only managed to shoot Lacerda in the foot, but an investigation revealed that the would-be assassin was Vargas's loyal bodyguard. Rather than leave office in disgrace, Vargas committed suicide in 1954.

Dictatorship and Democracy

Juscelino Kubitschek

Juscelino Kubitschek, a former governor of the state of Minas Gerais, succeeded to the presidency by open election in 1955. Over the next few years, Brazil developed into Latin America's industrial powerhouse. The immense Itaipú Dam, on the border with Paraguay, supplied hydroelectricity to fuel new auto, steel, and manufacturing businesses. Brazil also undertook nuclear power projects in cooperation with the United States. New roads were built across Amazonia and western Brazil, and Kubitschek's pet project, the new national capital of Brasília, rose in the hinterlands, 600 miles (965 km) from the seacoast. But when Kubitschek left office in 1961, Brazil was caught in an inflationary crisis, with prices rising rapidly and many workers threatened by poverty and hunger. Demonstrations erupted in many cities as workers and poor farmers angrily demanded economic and social reform.

The Brazilian military still exercised a powerful influence on the political scene. Military leaders saw the unrest as a dire threat to their country and greatly feared a Communist revolution. Communist guerrilla movements were growing in many Latin American nations, and a Communist-led revolution had already occurred in Cuba. In 1964 a junta (committee) of Brazilian military officers seized power after the president, João Goulart, began nationalizing companies and establishing ties with Communist countries, including Cuba. The armed forces promptly banned strikes and demonstrations and imprisoned many union leaders. The police ransacked left-wing newspapers and the homes of resisters, and libraries were inspected for Communistic books. Brazil's new regime used intimidation and propaganda to teach unconditional patriotism. Government agents tortured and abused anyone who resisted or opposed the government.

The military welcomed foreign corporations to Brazil, and the country's economy boomed from 1967 to 1973. But benefits were seen only by the rich. The gap between rich and poor, which had always been wide, stretched even further. Laborers were forced to work for extremely low wages. By the end of the 1970s, foreign debt had grown to $64.2 billion, and the Brazilian public began to blame the country's growing social and economic problems on the military's control of the presidency, which was bringing corruption scandals as well as mismanagement. A new law and the policy of *abertura* (opening) ended restrictions on opposition political parties in 1979, yet the public criticism persisted.

In January 1985, an alliance of opposition parties known as the Partido Frente Liberal (Liberal Front Party), led by Senator Tancredo Neves, claimed victory in a presidential election, and the government returned to civilian control. But Neves died in April 1985, just days before his inauguration, and Vice President José Sarney took the oath instead. The new president's finance ministers devised plans to slash government spending and control wages and prices in order to stabilize the currency, but Sarney's term ultimately brought more economic instability. In December 1989, the people voted Sarney out of office, replacing him with Fernando Collor de Mello.

Itamar Franco was elected in 1992. His finance minister, Fernando Henrique Cardoso, worked out the Real Plan, which froze prices and established a new currency, the real, which was pegged to the U.S. dollar in value.

As part of the Real Plan, all private bank accounts in Brazil were temporarily frozen. This drastic measure created a simmering resentment among ordinary Brazilians, who still looked on their government with cynicism and mistrust. The Real Plan did stem the inflation that had ravaged the country's economy, but unemployment remained high, especially in cities already teeming with poor refugees from the countryside. Although his innovations brought him the presidency in 1994, and reelection in 1998, Cardoso still faces a struggling economy. He also must deal with a political system made chaotic by the interaction of many contending, small parties. Each of these parties has an interest in addressing regional concerns, making a coordinated nationwide effort all the more difficult.

Government

The constitution of October 5, 1988, the eighth in Brazil's history, makes the president of Brazil the country's ceremonial head of state and the most powerful figure in the federal government. This constitution

Fernando Henrique Cardoso reviews the honor guard after being sworn in following his reelection as president of Brazil in 1998. To learn more about the president and about Brazil's elections, go to vgsbooks.com for links.

did not resolve a long-standing debate over the final form of Brazil's government, however. In 1993 the nation held a plebiscite (a national vote on an important issue). Voters could vote for a presidential system (in which the executive is separate from the legislature and elected by the citizens), a parliamentary system (in which executive power is held by a prime minister who is part of—and selected by—the legislature), or a return to a constitutional monarchy. Voters chose a presidential system.

The president has broad powers to introduce legislation and devise domestic and foreign policy, and runs the government through a cabinet of ministers which he or she appoints. Rather than representing political differences, such as liberal versus conservative, Brazil's eight major parties originate in specific regions and usually represent the local interests of these regions.

A two-house national congress comprises the legislative branch of government. The eighty-one-member Senate includes three members from each state and from the federal district that includes the capital of Brasília. While senators serve eight-year terms, members of the Chamber of Deputies serve for four years. There are 513 members of this lower house, elected by proportional representation, in which each political party is granted a number of seats corresponding to the percentage of the popular vote it has won. Local elections are held two years after the presidential elections.

The highest court in Brazil is the Supreme Federal Tribunal. Like all judges in Brazil, the eleven judges of the Tribunal serve for life, or until they retire, and are not allowed to hold any other employment. Below the Supreme Federal Tribunal is the Higher Tribunal of Justice as well as federal tribunals in each region, and state tribunals. Brazil also has lower courts with jurisdiction in labor, election, and military cases.

THE PEOPLE

Brazil's population reached an estimated 171.8 million by mid-2001. Overall, there are an average of 52 people in every square mile (20 people per sq. km) of the country, and about 78 percent of the people live in urban areas. Every state of Brazil, except for the state of Maranhão, has a predominantly urban population.

About 55 percent of the population descends from Portuguese and other European peoples, most significantly Italians, Germans, Spaniards, and Poles. A population of mixed African and European heritage makes up an additional 38 percent, while Afro-Brazilians constitute another 6 percent. Nearly all of Brazil's ethnic Asians—primarily Japanese—live in the urban areas and make up less than 1 percent of the population.

Brazil's population is heavily concentrated within 200 miles (320 km) of the east-central seacoast, the area of the country's earliest colonial settlements. The wave of immigration that began in the late nineteenth century also brought Europeans and Asians to Brazilian

port cities along the Atlantic. The westward movement of bandeirantes (explorers) and others followed a few well-defined routes into the subtropical and tropical forests of the interior. Over time, new arrivals from the eastern seaboard filled in the empty spaces between these routes with small farms and plantations. The Brazilian wilderness gradually retreated, although many remote areas of the country are still rarely traveled and completely unsettled.

Brazil's Indigenous Peoples

This westward migration decimated the indigenous tribes who, as the millions of colonists and immigrants arrived, pressed into the more inhospitable areas of Amazonia and western Brazil. By the end of the twentieth century, the indigenous population survived only in fragmented communities on small, state-owned reserves (land set aside for indigenous peoples). While it may have numbered as many as seven million individuals on the first arrival of Europeans, the indigenous population has been

Some **indigenous people** still live modest lives entirely separate from Brazilian society at large. To learn more about Brazil's diverse peoples, including the Yanomami and other ethnic groups, go to vgsbooks.com for links.

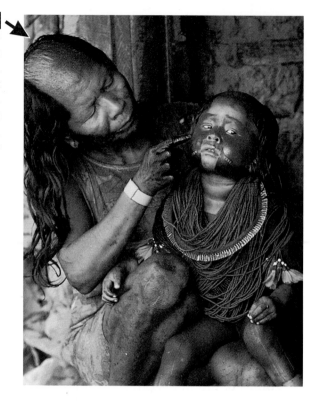

reduced to about 330,000, or less than one-quarter of 1 percent of the Brazilian nation.

Brazil has established 651 separate Indian reserves, home to about 230 different tribes. More than half of these groups live in the Amazon region, the homeland of the Yanomami, who live on a reserve of 23.7 million acres (9.6 million hectares). The Yanomami, the Guaraní, and about 10 percent of all indigenous peoples still live a hunter-gatherer existence, with many such people having no contact whatsoever with the Brazilian administration or the rest of Brazilian society.

By the constitution of Brazil, one-tenth of the country is to be set aside as reserves for indigenous peoples. These reserves are closed to exploitation by outsiders, but with their game and resources dwindling, many of the inhabitants still suffer poverty and malnutrition. There are few economic opportunities, and to survive, many reservation dwellers sell their crafts or household wares or cater to tourists as guides.

The establishment of reserves has not prevented encroachment on indigenous hunting grounds and villages, or the elimination of useful plants and animal species, such as the tapir (a short, thick animal that is related to the horse but looks more like a pig and is hunted for its meat and its hide). In search of fertile land, Brazilian farmers have cleared large swaths of rain forest, destroying the natural habitat of birds and game. In search of precious minerals, gold miners known as *garimpeiros* have denuded (stripped the surface layer of) forested hillsides and built dams and sluices along Amazonian waterways. The search for valuable resources has also brought violence, as entire villages have been massacred by those staking claims to land and minerals.

A Stratified Society

One of Brazil's most pressing problems has always been income disparity. The country's economic growth has gone hand in hand with the grinding poverty that afflicts more than a quarter of the population. The situation is at its worst in the northeast, a region largely bypassed by industrial development. The nine states of the northeastern region have an average per-capita income that is one-half of what it is in the southeastern and southern regions.

There are also disparities in income between men and women, and between nonwhite and white segments of the Brazilian population. Women earn on average less than two thirds of the wages earned by men, while nonwhite workers earn a little more than two-thirds of the average wage for whites.

The low wages paid to manual laborers force many Brazilian families to send their young children to work in order to survive. When labor precludes education—the key to a middle-class income—the cycle of poverty continues. The Brazilian poor also face a lack of adequate medical care, and approximately ten million people in the country are homeless.

Health

Brazil's birthrate is 22 births for every 1,000 people, and the country is growing at the rate of 1.5 percent every year. This figure represents a steady decline from the 1970s, when the growth rate in Brazil was 2.4 percent. Life expectancy has reached 65 years for males and 72 years for females, figures slightly lower than those for South America as a whole.

Infant mortality stands at 35 deaths per 1,000 live births, an average figure for South America, where the rate varies widely from a low of 10 in Chile to a high of 67 in Bolivia. Between 1970 and 1990, the mortality rate for children under five years old declined dramatically, a result of generally better health care and immunization against diseases such as diphtheria and measles. A more telling indicator of health problems, including malnutrition and scarce medical facilities, is the rate of maternal mortality—the percentage of women who die in childbirth—which in 1999 stood at 114 per 1,000 live births. This means that a Brazilian mother is almost three times more likely to die in childbirth than her baby.

Health problems in Brazil vary by region and by environment. The Amazon region, for example, is plagued with hundreds of thousands of cases of malaria. Spread by infected mosquitoes, malaria causes intense fever, exhaustion, delirium, and in some cases, death. The Amazon and the northeast regions suffer from other tropical diseases such as schistosomiasis, dengue fever, and yellow fever. Areas subject to seasonal flooding suffer outbreaks of cholera, an infectious disease that spreads through poor sanitation and that causes death through dehydration. The western Amazon suffers the highest rate of the liver disease hepatitis.

The southeast, the most urbanized region of the country, has 74 percent of Brazil's cases of AIDS (acquired immunodeficiency syndrome). The rate of AIDS cases in the country as a whole has reached 74 per 100,000 inhabitants, with three males for every female affected. Brazil has fought the AIDS epidemic with public education programs, which inform Brazilians how to prevent AIDS by avoiding risky behavior such as needle-sharing and unprotected sex. The results, however, have been discouraging. AIDS still poses a serious health risk to inhabitants of Brazilian cities, and the country suffers the highest number of AIDS cases in South America.

This sidewalk display for **International AIDS Day** features Brazilian soccer superstar Ronaldo Luiz Nazario da Lima. The posters say, "He protects his game."

Brazil has also scored important health victories, especially over childhood diseases. Polio disappeared from the country in 1989, and the number of measles cases declined sharply throughout the 1990s. Tetanus and diphtheria outbreaks still affect the northern and northeastern regions. Occasional measles outbreaks still occur in large urban areas, including São Paulo, a city that has also suffered outbreaks of encephalitis, hantavirus, and purpuric fever. Brazil also weathered a severe cholera outbreak in the early 1990s.

An important indicator of the slowly improving health conditions in Brazil is a decline in malnutrition. One important measure of malnutrition is the ratio of malnourished to obese children. From 1975 through 1989, that ratio declined from 4-to-1 down to 2-to-1. The average height of Brazilian children also increased by 1.8 inches (4.6 cm) from the 1960s to the 1980s. However, young Brazilians suffer high rates of accidents and homicide. Rising crime rates and increasing violence in urban Brazil have made homicide the leading cause of death among children between the ages of 15 and 19.

Education

The literacy rate of adults in Brazil is about 84 percent, although some adults considered literate can write little more than their own names. Still, the rate represents a steady improvement since 1950, when more than half of all Brazilians could not read or write at all, and is largely the result of compulsory and free primary schooling for Brazilians between the ages of seven and fourteen. Secondary school, which lasts for three years, begins at age fifteen.

The elementary schools in Brazil are crowded, and the average student receives only about four hours of instruction every day. Many students attend school for a few years, then drop out. Many parents, especially those in rural areas, need whatever extra income their children can bring into the household from work, and as a result enrollment in primary schools represents only 88 percent of the entire school-age population. Only about one-third of all primary students actually complete 8 years of school, and the average Brazilian gets about 6.3 years of education.

Brazil has seventy-seven public universities, which have been enrolling a steadily greater percentage of the country's post-secondary students. Each state has at least one state-owned federal university. Tuition is free, and the universities receive about 60 percent of the federal education budget. These institutions, however, suffer the same social stratification in the country as a whole. Enrollment, generally, is limited to members of the social elite and to those who have the ability to remain in school and complete their education.

CULTURAL LIFE

Brazilians like to describe their country as a work of art, a natural masterpiece. The mountains, rain forests, and magnificent seacoast do provide a dramatic setting. But the people enjoy human-made creativity above all, and especially the art of celebration. Brazilian festivals are well known around the world, as is a spirit of invention that goes beyond works of art, music, and literature. The people of Brazil appreciate nothing quite so much as a creative approach to everyday life and the many problems and challenges it can present.

▶ Television

Everyday problems provide the common stuff of *telenovelas*, or prime-time soap operas, which have captured a huge following among Brazilians. These dramas often deal with important political, social, and moral issues, giving them a significance beyond mere entertainment. They have made television the most popular communications medium in Brazil. There are several national networks, the largest of

which are SBT (Sistema Brasileiro de Televisão) and Globo, a network so wealthy and powerful that it has made and unmade many political careers and business fortunes. Globo's *Jornal Nacional*, which begins at 8:10 every evening, tops the ratings for news presentations. Morning network shows emphasize educational and juvenile programming, while talk shows dominate the afternoon airwaves.

Cable networks and digital or satellite systems compete with the networks, having captured about 10 percent of the total audience, a percentage that is steadily growing. A household with a satellite dish can tune in to as many as fifty stations from the United States, Europe, and the rest of Latin America. Specialized Brazilian cable stations cover sports, education, news, or culture.

◉ Music

A love of music cuts across all social and ethnic classes within Brazil, and the nation's music reflects its diverse heritage. Indigenous

Brazilians have a rich tradition of songs, dances, and musical instruments such as the *maracá*, a pebble-filled gourd of the Tupinamba people that clatters with a rhythmic buzz when shaken. The colonists brought European instruments, such as the guitar, violin, piano, accordion, and tambourine across the Atlantic, while African slaves brought their drums and percussion instruments as well as familiar dances such as the *jongo*, the *lundu*, and the samba.

Written Brazilian music began with a composer named Domingos Caldas Barbosa, who set down songs and dance music in the eighteenth century. In the next century, the musicians of Rio de Janeiro created *choro*, an improvisational version of popular European dance tunes performed on guitars, flutes, mandolins, clarinets, and a ukulele-like instrument known as the *cavaquinho*. Choro music is made up of several variations—sometimes slow and dignified, sometimes swinging and quick—written on a simple opening tune. Modern Brazilian musicians still perform and write choro, a jazzlike style that allows them to showcase their talent at composition as well as improvisation.

Choro had a strong influence on Heitor Villa-Lobos, Brazil's most famous classical composer, who started his career as a young choro performer. Villa-Lobos traveled widely in Brazil to learn the rhythms and instruments of indigenous and Afro-Brazilian musicians. He turned to Europe for inspiration as well, and his *Bachianas Brasileiras* represents a Brazilian-style tribute to Johann Sebastian Bach, a titan of European classical music.

After the emancipation of the slaves in 1888, African music, dance, and percussion gradually began to influence Brazilian popular music.

Heitor Villa-Lobos wrote classical music inspired by indigenous and Afro-Brazilian music.

A **capoeira dancer** dazzles his audience in Salvador, Brazil.

AFRO-BRAZILIAN CAPOEIRA

Capoeira is a blend of dance and martial art that originated with slaves who descended from the Bantu peoples of Angola and the rest of southern Africa. Originally a form of unarmed self-defense, capoeira has become a disciplined form of dance, an athletic ballet. Accompanied by a tambourine and a stringed instrument known as a *berimbaus*, capoeira contestants work in pairs, their legs and arms moving rapidly through poses and leaps, their hands sometimes wielding a pair of wooden sticks. Go to vgs-books.com for links to sites where you can learn more about capoeira.

African drums took the central place in music groups of all sizes. In 1917 a recorded song called "Pelo Telefone" touched off Brazil's long-lasting craze for samba music. A dance first imported by slaves, samba spread through radio, through gramophone recordings, and through the dancing and singing of Carnaval, an annual pre-Lenten festival that first took place in 1840 in Rio de Janeiro. The first samba schools were established in the late 1920s, allowing musicians to hone their skills at samba's lilting, complex rhythms and bittersweet melodies. An elaborate set of Carnaval customs and costumes developed alongside the music of nationally known *sambistas,* or samba composers.

Brazilian musicians carried samba and a catchy new rhythm known as bossa nova to the United States and Europe, beginning in the 1950s. Gilberto Gil, Antônio Carlos Jobim, and Sergio Mendes found a receptive audience among American jazz musicians such as Dizzy Gillespie and Gil Evans, who began to incorporate Brazilian percussion and rhythm into their works. Meanwhile, under the military dictatorship that began in the 1960s, music became a relatively safe form of protest and grievance. The song "Caminhando," by Geraldo Vandré, was adopted as a national anthem of resistance to the military regime.

Brazilian musicians enjoyed another wave of international popularity in the late 1990s. Afro-Brazilian bands, including Olodum and Timbalada, have sold millions of albums in the rest of Latin America and in Africa. Brazilian singer-songwriter Caetano Veloso reached a worldwide audience with his hit 1999 album *Livro*.

Literature and Art

Gregório de Mattos, who wrote biting satires of Brazil's colonial leaders in the seventeenth century, stands out as an early icon of Brazilian literature. Joaquim Maria Machado de Assis (1839–1908), a mixed-race Brazilian who wrote dramatic stories about the families of his home town of Rio de Janeiro, has become internationally renowned for *Philosopher or Dog, Dom Casmurro,* and *Epitaph of a Small Winner,* stories of the lives of families great and small. Antônio de Castro Alves, the son of a slave, rendered the hardships of slavery in his powerful books of poetry. One of the most famous works of Brazilian literature, *Os Sertões,* or *Rebellion in the Backlands.* This work by Euclides da Cunha presents a fictionalized account of a historical revolt in 1897, which was led by a religious visionary named Antônio Conselheiro. The real-life utopia that Conselheiro built and led in an impoverished corner of northern Brazil was destroyed by a military expedition, but it has survived as a symbol of justice and democracy in the national imagination.

The leading Brazilian writer of the twentieth century, Jorge Amado, described the harsh realities of agricultural workers and the poor of Bahia in his earlier books. His famous novel, which was also made into a film, *Dona Flor and Her Two Husbands* skewers the pompous pretensions of rural landowners. Amado died at age eighty-eight in 2001. His works have been translated into forty-eight languages.

One of Brazil's twentieth-century literary highlights was a diary entitled *Beyond All Pity,* the work of Carolina Maria de Jesus. This work, which described the daily life of the São Paulo slums, touched a responsive cord among Brazilians who recognize widespread urban poverty as their nation's toughest modern challenge.

In the field of the visual arts, Brazilians struggled for many years to escape the domination of European forms and styles. Antônio Francisco Lisboa, an eighteenth-century artist of Minas Gerais, is acclaimed for his imaginative architecture and sculpture. Two of his most famous works are the carvings in the Church of São Francisco at Ouro Prêto and the statues of the twelve prophets at Congonhas. Lisboa's works are all the more remarkable for the fact that this disabled artist did not have the use of his hands. According to tradition, he is said to have carved his works using a hammer and chisel bound to his forearms. Lisboa is more commonly known by the name Aleijadinho, or "Little Cripple."

In 1922, as young people in Brazil were becoming frustrated with conservative European influences on art, a painter named Emiliano Di Cavalcanti and several poets organized Modern Art Week in São Paulo. This festival of dance, poetry readings, and art exhibits introduced art's Modernist movement—a self-concious break with the past in search of new forms of expression—to Brazil.

Brazilian architecture has fought its own rebellion against the past. While colonial architecture marks the cities of Salvador and Ouro Prêto, the architect Oscar Niemeyer, a native of Rio de Janeiro, built an entire city of the future in Brasília. To reflect modern communications and industry, the city was designed in the shape of a jet airplane, with the long "fuselage" containing government buildings and "wings"

Completed in 1997, the **Museum of Contemporary Art** in Niterói is across Guanabara Bay from Rio de Janeiro. The futuristic building was designed by Oscar Niemeyer, who was also the lead architect of Brasília in the 1960s.

holding residential blocks. Brasília also offers residents sweeping lawns and parks. The ratio of 269 square feet (25 sq. m) of green space per resident is the one of the highest of all the world's major cities.

Religion

Settled in large part by the Catholic Portuguese and by a large contingent of Catholic missionaries and religious brotherhoods, Brazil has remained a Roman Catholic nation for five centuries. For many years, Brazil was the largest Roman Catholic nation in the world. In the late twentieth century, however, the Catholic religion suffered a steady decline in popularity among ordinary Brazilians. In 1960, 93 percent of all Brazilians considered themselves practicing Catholics, a statistic that dropped to about 80 percent by the 1990s. Of that number, only about ten million (about 14 percent) regularly attend a Catholic Mass, and a minority of Catholics follow the Church's teachings on such issues as divorce and birth control.

By contrast, Protestant and evangelical churches gained strength in the twentieth century. The Universal Church of the Kingdom of God claims about 3.5 million members, while the Jehovah's Witnesses and the Church of Jesus Christ of Latter-day Saints, whose followers are called Mormons, have come to Brazil from North America. Protestant churches together had attracted about 22 percent of the population by the mid-1990s. Substantial Jewish communities exist in São Paulo, Rio de Janeiro, and Pôrto Alegre. About 130,000 Jews lived in Brazil at the close of the twentieth century.

In the second half of the twentieth century, many Latin American pastors (mostly Roman Catholic clergy) confronted grinding poverty among their parishioners by forming a new understanding of their work. Believing that it was blasphemous to care for people's souls while ignoring their needs for food and shelter, these pastors began a new religious movement called liberation theology. By 1980 liberation theologists were doing missionary work in more than eighty thousand poor communities in Brazil. Pope John Paul II has criticized liberation theology and its followers, accusing them of wrongly supporting armed revolutions and promoting Marxist class-struggle concepts (that are considered antitraditional and anti-Catholic).

A variety of smaller sects have flourished in Brazil, including several based on African religion imported by slaves. Two of the most important Afro-Brazilian sects are *umbanda* and *candomblé*. Based on the beliefs brought by the Yoruba people of West Africa, candomblé was a way to carry on a secret religion for Brazilian slaves, who were often forbidden to practice their faiths. Traditional African gods were often worshipped in the guise of Catholic saints, including

Candomblé worshipers in Brazil sweep and wash around their church for one of the annual Iemanjá festivals. The ritual symbolizes cleansing of the soul for a new year. Visit vgsbooks.com for links to colorful photographs of other Brazilian festivals, including Carnaval, and take a quiz to see how much you've learned about Brazil.

Saint George (who stood for Ogum, the Yoruba god of war) and Saint Barbara (Yansã, the goddess of the winds). Candomblé also incorporated the animist beliefs of indigenous Brazilians, who recognized spirits in natural forces and features of the Amazonian forest. Candomblé is very strong in the state of Bahia.

Holidays and Festivals

The national holidays of Brazil include Tiradentes Day, celebrated on April 21, which commemorates the death of Joaquim José da Silva Xavier, or Tiradentes, the national hero of independence. Cities large and small hold parties and celebrations during the Festas Juninas, or June Festivals, which originated with the Catholic feasts of Saint John and Saint Peter. October 12 is the feast of Our Lady Aparecida, the patron saint of Brazil. The Brazilian Labor Day takes place on May 1, and Independence Day is on September 7.

The most important Christian holidays in Brazil are Easter and Christmas. On Christmas Eve, Brazilian families and friends exchange small gifts, while children wait expectantly for the presents brought by Papai Noel (Father Christmas) on Christmas Day. The Catholic faith also includes an elaborate calendar of festivals and local observances. A Festa do Divino, the Feast of the Holy Ghost, takes place fifty days after Easter in the town of Paraty, south of Rio de Janeiro. Great processions of church officials and townspeople wind through the streets, following a glittering image of the Holy Ghost. Participants bring traditional Holy Ghost flags to doorways to bless homes for the coming year. At the end of the procession, a boy is crowned as festival prince and the townspeople hand out sweets to children and meals to the poor.

All Brazilians prepare for the fasting and prayer of the Christian Lenten season (the forty days leading up to Easter) with Carnaval, an exuberant week of dancing, music, parades, and partying that takes over Rio de Janeiro and other Brazilian cities in the week before Ash Wednesday. The Brazilian Carnaval began with a masked ball in the imperial capital of Rio de Janeiro in 1840. The party imitated the *entrada*, a pre-Lenten celebration in Portugal. Over the years, Rio's Carnaval grew bigger and noisier until it became the largest such celebration in the world. During Carnaval, Brazilian mayors hand the keys of their cities over to Momo, an ancient Greek king of celebration and jokes. Street parades, masked balls, and great public bonfires attract Brazilians who, for a short time, completely escape the cares of daily life. For three straight nights, students of the samba schools of Brazil dress up in fantastically colored costumes—many of them representing the mythical creatures of folklore—and parade past crowds of onlookers, who join in with drumming, singing, shouting, and exuberant dancing along the city's crowded and noisy streets.

The festival of Bois de Parintins takes place in late June on Tupinambarana, an Amazonian island. Two competing sides—the "red" and the "blue"—gather in a large *bumbódromo*, a temporary stadium, to sing and dance to *toada de boi*, a musical style that was born in the forests along the Amazon River but is catching on throughout Brazil. The story of the *boi-bumbá* dance describes the killing of an ox by a Brazilian cowboy for the sake of the woman he loves. The songs and tales performed during the Bois de Parintins festival tell how the ox miraculously comes back to life.

New Years' Eve is celebrated with parties and parades all over the country. Followers of the Afro-Brazilian cults such as candomblé celebrate one of the festivals of Iemanjá, the mother of waters, on the evening of the last day of the year. At midnight, crowds of thousands—practitioners and onlookers as well—approach the seashore with offerings of flowers, wreaths, perfume, food, drink, and other gifts that are cast into the sea with prayers for good luck in the coming year.

◉ Sports

Many would claim the sport of *futebol*, or soccer, as Brazil's true national religion. The soccer clubs of Brazil represent much more than sports teams. They are huge social clubs that command the loyalty of millions of people from their hometown and home state who suffer with losses and celebrate victories. Most are operated by amateur managers and have been in existence for at least seventy years. On the day of a match, the home team's colors can be seen in clothing, on pennants, in storefront displays, and even in the wrapping for gifts exchanged by friends and family.

For much of the twentieth century, the national soccer team of Brazil was recognized as the best in the world. Brazil has won four World Cups, the competition held every four years among the best teams in the world (through a long series of qualifying matches). Brazil is the only country in the world that has qualified for every World Cup tournament. Important World Cup matches are occasions for closing stores and businesses and retiring in front of a television or radio set.

Much of Brazil's fame as a soccer powerhouse rests on the legendary abilities of Pelé. Edson Arantes do Nascimento (his real name) was of medium height but had astounding kicking strength and an uncanny ability to anticipate opponents' moves. After retiring from professional soccer, he served as Brazil's minister of sports from 1977 to 1999, promoting soccer and athletics around the world.

Pelé *(# 10, right)* is widely held to be the best soccer player of all time.

There are several other popular team sports in Brazil besides soccer. All move at a fast pace and don't include many stops in the action. (Baseball, American football, golf, and cricket—slow games by Brazilian standards—never gained a following among Brazilians, either as spectators or participants.) Indoor soccer, which was created by Brazilians, grew into an international sport in the 1990s. Brazilians also follow national volleyball and basketball teams, which have won several international championships over the years.

The fastest sport of all, auto racing, has millions of avid followers among Brazilians. The country is internationally famous for its daring and sometimes reckless drivers, who love to imitate Brazil's many Formula One champions.

Food

Throughout Brazil, the staple foods are bread, rice, beans, cheese, eggs, and meat. The Brazilian day begins with *café com leite,* or coffee with milk, and bread and fruit. The largest meal of the day is eaten for lunch, but this meal varies from north to south within Brazil. In the north, a typical big meal will consist of rice, fish, salad, and fruit. Farther south, meat is presented more commonly than fish, along with beans, rice, potatoes, and salad. Lighter dinners may include soup, bread, and a dessert of coffee and pastry.

One of the best-known Brazilian meals is a stew called *feijoada,* created by Brazilian slaves who had to rely on food left over from their owners' tables. The modern feijoada includes black beans, rice, sausages, and slices of pork, mixed with a sauce either spicy or mild and often eaten with orange slices. *Tutu de feijão* varies from the more common dish by adding a ground-up spice powder. Favorite vegetable side dishes include yams, squash, peppers, beans, and peanuts. French fries are served along with meat in the dish known as *bife com fritas.* The Brazilian barbecue called *churrasco* originated in the south and is a favorite dish in Rio de Janeiro. Churrasco may include a wide variety of different meats and is often served *rodízio*-style on skewers.

The colonial-era staple of manioc has survived in modern Brazil as *farinha de manioca,* or manioc flour, an ingredient in several dishes. Manioc, sweet potato, and palm oil are the basic ingredients in the cuisine of Bahia, where cooks add African spices to their famous seafood dishes, including *abará* (shrimp and beans served like a tamale in a banana skin) and *vatapá,* a thick and spicy soup of coconut milk, ginger, and shrimp. Other favored fish dishes are *tambaqui, dourado,* and *pirarucu,* an enormous freshwater fish whose thick flesh, according to many, tastes like chicken.

FEIJOADA*

2 cups black beans

4 cups water

1 ham bone or pork hock

1 teaspoon salt

1/2 teaspoon pepper

8 pork sausage links or hot dogs

2 cups rice

1 orange, sliced

1. Rinse beans thoroughly in cold water. In a large, covered pot, add enough water to cover beans. Soak overnight.

2. Drain beans and add 4 cups fresh water, ham bone or pork hock, salt, and pepper.

3. Bring to a boil, then reduce heat, cover, and simmer over low heat for 3 hours.

4. Brown pork links, cut in bite-sized pieces, and add to the bean mixture. If using hot dogs, cut them into bite-sized pieces and add directly to the bean mixture. Heat thoroughly.

5. Serve with rice and orange slices.

*Vary this Brazilian favorite by adding other kinds of meat such as smoked beef tongue, smoked pork ribs, or other cuts of pork.

As refreshments or with meals, Brazilians drink fruit juices, lemonade, milk, and soft drinks. In a country whose coffee beans are exported all over the world, Brazilians have naturally taken to coffee drinking—at all times of the day. In the south, the drink known as maté, a strong herbal tea, also has its fans.

THE ECONOMY

Through the mid-twentieth century, Brazil boasted one of the fastest-growing economies in the world. But high debts and inflation took a heavy toll in later years. In 1989 alone, wage earners lost 20 percent of their buying power as the currency lost much of its value. To stabilize the Brazilian currency, the government attempted to curb public spending in the early 1990s. In 1992 Brazil also convinced its foreign creditors to reschedule its heavy debts.

But these programs were hurt by the resignation of President Fernando Collor de Mello, who left office in 1992 under a cloud of scandal. By the middle of 1994, inflation in Brazil was running at 50 percent, and the prices of food and household goods were rising steeply—sometimes every day.

The main problem was government spending. Because the government owned and operated so many important industries—such as utilities, automobile and aircraft manufacturers, and telecommunications companies—it was spending a tremendous amount of money. And

because these industries did not have to make a profit to stay in business, they were running inefficiently and wasting money. As the government printed more money to provide for its own spending, the value of Brazilian currency fell, and workers saw their salaries buying less and less in the marketplace.

In an attempt to get the currency under control, Brazil devised an entirely new monetary unit, known as the real, and pegged its value directly to the U.S. dollar. When the dollar rose or fell, the real moved in tandem, and since the dollar is a fairly stable and strong currency, this action increased confidence in Brazilian money.

The Plano Real (Real Plan) successfully reduced inflation to a rate of 7.2 percent in 1997. This made it easier for Brazilian workers to purchase food and other necessities. It also greatly improved Brazil's standing in the eyes of foreign investors, who tend to avoid nations with unmanageable debts, high inflation, and weak currencies. Investment in Brazilian companies steadily increased into the twenty-first century.

To get public spending under control, the government sold off state-owned industrial, energy, and communications companies. The privatization had two goals: first, to increase efficiency by running these businesses as private enterprises, which would have to make a profit to survive; and second, to reduce government spending, which was crippling the country's ability to invest in other areas, such as health, education, and welfare programs.

But slashing public spending has also resulted in hardship for those dependent on unemployment compensation and publicly subsidized medical care, a situation that has worsened many of the social ills that plague Brazil's poor. And it has been only partially successful, as continuing budget deficits have increased the country's public debt load even further.

In 1998 an international economic crisis began, during which many Latin American currencies fell sharply in value. When foreign investment dried up, the country then abandoned the original Real Plan. It devalued the real by 8 percent, then declared that the currency would be allowed to float in value. The government hopes this measure will address outsiders' concerns that the currency was overvalued.

> **"Don't abandon Brazil; help it to change."** So goes one government slogan in Brazil's battle against emigration. As economic conditions worsen in Brazil, more and more citizens are leaving the country to seek better opportunities, a situation Brazilian authorities fear will lead to a brain drain.

Brazil's government also has tried to address the issue of income disparity. The wealthiest 10 percent of the nation's population earns about half of Brazil's income, while the lowest 10 percent earns about 1 percent. This income disparity, which results from centuries of social stratification and the traditional control of the Brazilian economy by a small elite of Brazilian society, poses a serious threat to political stability and to economic growth.

◉ Industry

The most advanced industrial nation in Latin America, Brazil has developed traditional heavy industries—such as mining, steelmaking, and auto production—as well as high-tech manufacturing. Traditionally, aircraft and aviation components provided the leading edge for technological innovation in Brazil, which claims the largest aerospace industry in Latin America and the fourth-largest in the world. In addition to iron, steel, and automobiles, Brazil exports military aircraft, helicopter components, and aircraft engines. The country also produces a wide range of civilian aircraft, including the EMB 120, a small commuter plane that has users around the world.

Auto manufacturing led Brazil's rapid economic growth of the 1960s and 1970s but suffered a severe downturn in the 1980s. The 1990s brought a complete recovery, thanks to higher import duties on imported cars. In the early 2000s, auto manufacturers were producing more than two million new cars every year, making this the largest single industrial sector in Latin America.

Brazil has long been a global center of shoe manufacturing. Brazilian factories also produce textiles, clothing, and appliances. Heavy and light industry employs about 20 percent of the workforce and produces about 36 percent of the country's total output.

Workers assemble small passenger planes at the Embraer plant in São Jose dos Campos.

◉ Agriculture

A nation founded on cash crops such as sugar, coffee, and tobacco, Brazil remains a self-sufficient producer and an important exporter of food to the rest of the world. At the end of the twentieth century, agriculture employed about 23 percent of the population and produced about 9 percent of the country's gross domestic product. Brazil remains an important supplier of grain, tobacco, sugar, soybeans, rice, and citrus fruits and is the world's largest producer of bananas, coffee, and orange juice. Livestock also provides valuable export income, and Brazil is home to the world's largest commercial herd of cows. Most of the nation's productive farmland lies in the southern and central regions, as the farms of northern Brazil must cope with light rainfall and periodic severe droughts.

There are serious social and environmental problems associated with farming in Brazil. Large plantations dominate agriculture in the backlands, where the population is sharply divided between landowners and the landless. By some estimates, there are five million landless farmers in Brazil who don't have the means to acquire their own plots, become financially independent, and improve their standard of living. Calls for reform of land policies have been answered by a government program of expropriation, in which land deemed unproductive by the government is taken from its owners and redistributed to farmers who have no land of their own. About 22 million acres (about 8 million hectares) have changed hands in this way, and more than 130,000 families have settled on new acreages of their own.

Unfortunately, opening up new lands to farming often brings environmental destruction. The slash-and-burn method of clearing the land, and logging for mahogany and other valuable hardwoods, are causing the slow but steady disappearance of the Amazonian rain forest. Cattle pastures and plots of wheat,

ECOTOURISM VS. DEFORESTATION

Brazil is nourishing a new business to help its economy and protect the Amazon region: ecotourism. The Amazon is already attracting tourists from around the world who hire local guides to learn about the rain forest and to journey up the river. Tourists visit remote villages, buy crafts made by the locals, and stay in hotels that range from luxurious to primitive. The government is trying to convince landowners that they can make more money by attracting visitors than by destroying it for other purposes. To learn more about ecotourism, go to vgsbooks.com for links.

tobacco, and other crops have replaced the dense forest, driving out many species of plants and animals. The process accelerates with new road projects. The Transamazon Highway, begun in the 1970s, was designed to cut across the Amazon Basin from the Atlantic coast to the Peruvian border and to enable poor farmers from the northeast to resettle in the region to improve their lives. However, only a portion of the highway was completed. Rains have washed away large sections of the road, and what remains is essentially impassable during the rainy season, which lasts from November to April.

Energy and Mining

Brazil's immense river system has played a crucial role in the country's energy self-sufficiency. The Itaipú Dam on the Paraná River has a capacity of more than 100,000 megawatts—enough power to electrify most of South America. By the first decade of the twenty-first century, hydropower provided more than 90 percent of the country's electricity. Thermal power makes up about 5 percent of energy production, and nuclear power about 1 percent.

Oil production reached about 1.5 million barrels per day in 2000. Several immense oil rigs have been built to extract oil from the large Campos basin, lying off the coast of southeastern Brazil. The country still must import roughly half of its oil from foreign sources to meet its needs. Petrobrás, the largest company in Brazil, produces oil and natural gas from land as well as offshore wells. To reduce dependence on imported oil, Brazil also has worked to become the world leader in the production of alcohol-based gasoline, a cleaner energy source that is manufactured from the native sugarcane and that powers most new Brazilian automobiles.

Mining in Brazil provided about 1 percent of Brazil's GDP (gross domestic product) in 1998. Brazil is home to the world's largest iron mine, as well as mining operations for gold and other precious

Mine workers in hard hats size up the day's work at the top of a gold mine shaft in Brazil.

minerals. The private company Companhia Vale do Rio Doce (CVRD) is the third-largest mining company in the world and Brazil's largest exporter. The company mines and exports 20 percent of the world's iron ore production, as well as gold, tin, and other minerals. Brazil also produces uranium, manganese, and copper.

Foreign Trade

Foreign trade steadily increased into the early twenty-first century, with the country running a small trade deficit, meaning Brazilians bought more from foreign countries than they exported. Along with currency reform and lower public spending, Brazil relaxed the duties it had charged on imports, an action that stimulated its trade with foreign countries, particularly with its neighbors in South America. The most important imports are machinery, electrical equipment, chemicals, oil, and electricity. The United States is the largest source of all imported goods, which total almost $50 billion annually.

Exports from Brazil average about $47 billion. The country's export business has suffered somewhat from the Real Plan, as the stronger currency made Brazilian-made goods more expensive on world markets. Brazil is still an important source of the world's agricultural commodities, including sugar, coffee, orange juice, soybeans, and cocoa. The United States is the nation's largest single customer, buying about 23 percent of all Brazilian exports. About 11 percent of Brazilian exports go to Asia, 28 percent to the rest of Latin America, 29 percent to the European Union countries, and 4 percent to the Middle East.

There is also an underside of Brazil's foreign trade. The nation, and particularly the Amazon basin, has become an important producer of coca leaves, which supply cocaine refineries and a market for illegal drugs in the United States and Europe. The Brazilian military has been enlisted in the effort to close down production and trafficking of illegal drugs.

As of January 1, 1995, Brazil became a partner in Mercosul, or the Southern Common Market. Argentina, Paraguay, and Uruguay are also partners. Mercosul provides its four member countries with a common trading market, which provides for

Since joining Mercosul, Brazil has developed such a strong relationship with its Spanish-speaking South American neighbors that the Brazilian senate has voted to make Spanish classes required in Brazil's public schools. In turn, Argentina has plans to teach Portuguese.

Brazil's economy minister, Pedro Malan *(left)*, leans over to speak with his Argentinean counterpart, Domingo Cavallo *(right)*, at a **Mercosul meeting** in São Paulo.

lower tariffs on goods crossing their borders. Mercosul has stimulated Brazilian exports and has made Argentina Brazil's second most important trading partner.

Transportation

Modern highways link Brazil's major cities, and paved roads have been built into the remote regions of Amazonia, making much of the region accessible. Maintaining the road system has been a drain on the nation's public treasury, however, at a time when cutbacks in public spending have been a priority. About 1 million miles (1.6 million km) of roadway, of which about 10 percent is paved, crisscross the country. Many regions continue to be inaccessible by road or railway, however, and Brazil has still not built any passable routes to its northern neighbors.

The automotive age has created its share of problems in Brazil. Poorly maintained roads and disregard of traffic laws have brought a high rate of accidents. In addition, endless traffic jams in the large cities cause pollution, noise, and considerable wasted time.

The rail network includes 18,600 miles (30,000 km) of track, of which 1,330 miles (2,140 km) are electrified. The Brazilian railroad system, known as the Rede Ferroviaria Federal (RFFSA), operates passenger and cargo trains. This public company lost money for many years before it was privatized in 1995 as part of the government's economic reform program.

A network of commuter, regional, and international airlines is essential to transportation in this large country. Brazil has ten airports open to international flights. The largest commercial aviation company is Varig. Brazil's export business also depends on the country's thirty-six seaports. Each year, hundreds of foreign cargo ships and

Manaus, Brazil, has a busy car ferry port on the Amazon River. Steamships on the Amazon can navigate the entire length of the river as far as Iquitos, Peru—2,287 miles (3,680 km) from the Atlantic Ocean.

tankers call at the port of Santos, near São Paulo, the largest and busiest port in South America.

In Amazonia, steamboats still provide the main form of transportation. Oceangoing steamships navigate the Amazon River with cargo and passengers.

Media and Communications

Brazil has about three hundred commercial television stations, as well as public stations used for educational broadcasting. Five private networks operate most of the private stations, with the largest of these the Globo (Rede Globo de Televisão) system. TV Educativa carries documentaries and educational programs.

Telephone communications have yet to reach outside of Brazilian cities. Subscribers must pay high fees and wait, sometimes for months, to have phone lines installed in their homes. Telebrás, the government telephone monopoly, became private in the late 1990s. As a result of the inefficient and expensive service, cell phones have become a popular means of private communications.

The newspapers of Brazil publish an ongoing and lively debate on current issues. Each is affiliated with a certain political stance: for example, *O Globo* and *Jorno do Brasil* of Rio de Janeiro are conservative, while *Fôlha de São Paulo* is leftist, and the *Gazeta* of São Paulo is a purely business newspaper. The most popular news magazines include *Manchete* and *Veja*.

For information as well as entertainment, Brazilians also turn to the Internet. Although only a small percentage of households have access to this medium, most Brazilians can make use of Internet cafés, located in most large towns and cities, as well as sidewalk Internet booths, which charge the public the equivalent of about one dollar for fifteen online minutes.

The Future

Brazil enters the twenty-first century with mixed prospects for the future. The Brazilian government must cope with many difficult social and economic problems. While natural resources, industry, and agriculture provide plentiful goods within the country and a brisk foreign trade, poverty and hunger plague rural areas as well as urban shantytowns. A product of the country's historic social inequalities, poverty has become self-sustaining, as families unable to afford education for their children force them into poorly paid jobs in which they cannot advance. University education remains a privilege of a social elite, and those without the money or connections to attain advanced degrees cannot make their way up the economic ladder. The low wages paid for most jobs dampen demand for consumer goods, while chaotic economic conditions make business ventures risky.

The Real Plan did manage to tame the inflation that raged in the 1980s and early 1990s, allowing Brazil to attract much-needed foreign investment. If managed and developed wisely, the country's natural resources can also help Brazil to improve its economic prospects. But the hardest work will be transforming a stratified and unequal society into one where opportunity and hope reach the millions of people who had neither at the close of the twentieth century.

This **samba school** takes its enthusiasm for computer technology to the streets for Carnaval in Rio de Janeiro.

10,000 B.C. Hunter-gatherers inhabit the coasts and river valleys of Brazil.

1900 B.C. Corn is cultivated by indigenous Brazilians and manioc is developed shortly afterward.

A.D. 400 Tupi-Guarani tribes invade coastal agricultural tribes and drive them away from the coast.

1419 Prince Dom Henrique (Henry the Navigator) begins sending ships to explore the western coast of Africa.

1494 The Treaty of Tordesillas establishes a boundary line between Spanish and Portuguese claims in the New World.

1500 Pedro Álvars Cabral sights the eastern coast of Brazil, which he calls Terra da Vera Cruz, and claims the territory for Portugal.

1530s The first African slaves arrive in Brazil.

1532 The first Portuguese colony is founded at São Vicente.

1534 Brazil is divided into fifteen hereditary territories known as captaincies.

1554 A Jesuit mission is established at São Paulo.

1565 Portuguese captain Estácio de Sá founds Rio de Janeiro.

1630 The Palmares quilombo, a refuge for escaped and freed slaves, is established in what is now Alagoas state in the northeast.

1654 The Portuguese expel Dutch colonists from Brazil.

1695 Gold is discovered in the Minas Gerais region, touching off a population boom in southeastern Brazil. The Palmares quilombo is overrun and destroyed.

1727 First coffee plants are brought to Brazil from French Guiana, and the first coffee plantations are built.

1750 Spain and Portugal settle their boundary disputes in South America by the Treaty of Madrid.

1759 The Jesuits are banished from Brazil.

1763 The Brazilian capital moves from Salvador to Rio de Janeiro.

1792 A plot to overthrow Portuguese rule ends with the execution of Tiradentes, who becomes a national hero.

1805 Aleijandinho finishes statues of the Twelve Prophets in Congonhas.

1808 Threatened by a French invasion under Napoleon, the regent of Portugal, João, and his court flee to Brazil.

1822   Brazil declares independence from Portugal. Pedro I, the son of King João VI of Portugal, is declared the emperor of Brazil.

1824   Brazil ratifies its first constitution as an independent state.

1840   The first Brazilian Carnaval is celebrated.

1865   Brazil joins the Triple Alliance with Argentina and Uruguay and declares war on Paraguay.

1888   Pedro II abolishes slavery by decree.

1889   Pedro II abdicates, and a republic is founded.

1892   A Rio de Janeiro zookeeper holds the first lottery game known as *jogo do bicho*.

1896   An elaborate opera house opens in Manaus during a boom in rubber production.

1917   Brazil joins the Allies fighting against Germany in Europe. The song "Pelo Telefone" is released, launching the samba craze.

1930   Getulio Vargas seizes power after a contested presidential election.

1937   Vargas establishes a new dictatorship under the name of Estado Novo (New State).

1942   Brazil joins the Allies in World War II.

1954   President Vargas commits suicide.

1960   The new capital of Brasília is inaugurated.

1964   The armed forces of Brazil stage a coup against the civilian government of João Goulart.

1975   Construction begins on the Itaipú Dam, to be completed in 1991.

1977   Pelé retires from soccer.

1985   Brazil's military dictatorship ends. José Sarney becomes the first civilian president in twenty one years.

1994   President Itamar Franco introduces the Real Plan to stabilize Brazil's currency.

1997   SIVAM project (the Amazon Surveillance System) begins.

1998   Fernando Henrique Cardoso becomes only the second president since 1930 to complete his term and is reelected.

2000   Brazilians celebrate the five-hundred-year anniversary of Pedro Álvars Cabral's landing at Brazil. The Bolshoi Ballet of Russia opens its first school outside of Russia in Joinville, Brazil.

2002   More than 70,000 people are infected and 28 people die in Brazil's worst recorded epidemic of dengue, a virus carried by mosquitoes.

COUNTRY NAME Federative Republic of Brazil

AREA 3,286,488 square miles (8,511,965 sq. km)

MAIN LANDFORMS Amazon Basin, Pantanal, sertão, Brazilian Highlands, Iguaçu Falls, Guiana Highlands

HIGHEST POINT Pico da Bandeira, 9,495 feet (2,894 m) above sea level

LOWEST POINT sea level

MAJOR RIVERS Amazon River, Paraná River, São Francisco River

ANIMALS Half of all species on earth live in Brazil, including howler monkeys, boa constrictors, scarlet macaws, anteaters, and capybaras.

CAPITAL CITY Brasília

OTHER MAJOR CITIES Belo Horizonte, Manaus, Rio de Janeiro, Salvador, São Paulo

OFFICIAL LANGUAGE Portuguese

MONETARY UNIT The real. 100 centavos = 1 real

BRAZILIAN CURRENCY

The Central Bank of Brazil was created December 31, 1964, and became the currency issuing bank for the nation. Brazil's old currency, the cruzeiro, was destroyed by many years of inflation, and after a new currency known as the real was introduced in 1994, the economic situation began to improve. The real breaks down into 100 centavos. Brazilian coins come in denominations of 1 real, and 1, 5, 10, and 50 centavos. Notes can be found in 1, 5, 10, 50, and 100 real amounts.

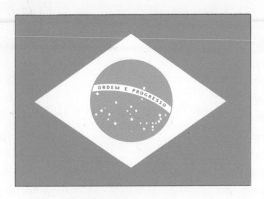

The Brazilian flag's background is a field of green, representing the country's forests and fertile plains. In the center of the flag lies an elongated yellow diamond, which represents the country's natural wealth in gold. The diamond holds a blue globe. Twenty-seven stars appear on the sphere, each standing for one of Brazil's twenty-six states and for the federal district. The stars stand in their position as seen from Rio de Janeiro on November 15, 1889, the day that Brazil became a republic. A banner crossing the globe reads Ordem e Progresso, Portuguese for "Order and Progress."

Flag

National Anthem

Brazil's national anthem was originally composed for a military band by Francisco Manuel da Silva, perhaps in 1841 (no one knows for sure). In 1922, verses written by Joaquim Osório Duque Estrada in 1909 were officially adopted. Shown below are the first three verses of the English translation.

The peaceful banks of the Ypiranga
Heard the resounding cry of an heroic people,
And the dazzling rays of the sun of Liberty
Bathed our country in their brilliant light.

If with strong arm we have succeeded
In winning a pledge of equality,
In thy bosom, O Liberty,
Our hearts will defy death itself!

O adored Fatherland,
Cherished and revered,
All Hail! All Hail!

Want to listen to Brazil's national anthem? Go to vgsbooks.com for a link.

JORGE AMADO (1912–2001) A twentieth-century author born in Itabuna, he was Brazil's best-known novelist. His books include *Dona Flor and Her Two Husbands* and *Os Sertões*.

TARSILA DO AMARAL (1886–1973) A native of São Paulo, Amaral was one of the most innovative and influential painters in Latin America in the early twentieth century. Her paintings were characterized by colorful and bold forms.

PEDRO ÁLVARS CABRAL (1467–1520) This sea captain and explorer was born in Belmonte, Portugal. In 1500 he and his crew became the first Europeans to see the coast of Brazil.

CAROLINA MARIA DE JESUS (1914–1977) An Afro-Brazilian woman born in the rural interior of Brazil, Jesus overcame impoverishment and published her diary, *Quarto de Despejo,* which became the best-selling book in Brazilian history.

ANTÔNIO CARLOS JOBIM (1927–1994) A Brazilian musician born in Rio de Janeiro, Jobim composed a hit song of the 1950s, "The Girl from Ipanema," which started a craze for Brazilian bossa nova music in the United States.

ANTÔNIO FRANCISCO LISBOA (1738–1814) Known as Aleijadinho, this eighteenth-century sculptor was born in Minas Gerais. He created expressive religious statuary in wood and soapstone.

CHICO MENDES (1944–1988) A union organizer in his home state, the western state of Acre, Mendes led demonstrations and blockades in Amazonia to prevent cattle ranchers from clearing rubber forests that provided a livelihood for Brazilian rubber tappers. Mendes was murdered by a cattle-rancher's son in 1988.

CARMEN MIRANDA (1909–1955) Born Maria do Carmo Miranda da Cunha in Marco de Canavezes, Portugal, she was raised in Rio de Janeiro. Miranda brought the samba to Hollywood and the United States and made this Brazilian dance popular all over the world.

MILTON NASCIMENTO (b. 1942) Born in Rio de Janeiro, Milton Nascimento is a popular jazz and pop musician whose music is appreciated all over the world. He has released nearly thirty albums and has been labeled by the *New York Times* as "one of the greatest musicians alive." Nascimento won a Grammy for Best Contemporary Pop Album for his 1999's album *Crooner* at the first annual Latin Grammy Awards in 2000.

OSCAR NIEMEYER (b. 1907) This architect, born in Rio de Janeiro, planned the futuristic capital of Brasília and designed many of

Brasília's monumental public buildings in the 1960s. Earlier, Niemeyer contributed to the design of the United Nations complex in New York City, completed in 1950. He continues to be known for his use of and innovations in concrete, glass, and steel such as the Museum of Contemporary Art in Niterói, completed in 1997.

PELÉ (b. 1940) Born Edson Arantes do Nascimento in Tres Coracoes, he is acknowledged around the world as the greatest soccer player of all time. Pelé scored 1,279 official goals during his career and played an important role in three of Brazil's four World Cup victories. As Minister of Sports, Pelé traveled around the world and became the best-known and most popular Brazilian diplomat abroad.

ALBERTO SANTOS-DUMONT (1873–1932) This inventor and engineer, born in the state of Minas Gerais, was popularly known in Brazil as the "father of aviation." Educated in Paris, France, Dumont built several different models of early airplanes and succeeded in short flights before the Wright Brothers accomplished the same thing in the United States.

AYERTON SENNA (1960–1994) Legendary Formula One race car driver, Ayerton Senna won an astonishing 25 percent of his races. Born in a São Paulo suburb, Senna was Formula One champion in 1988, 1990, and 1991. He was killed when his car hit the wall going 200 miles per hour (320 kph) during the 1994 San Marino Grand Prix in Italy.

JOAQUIM JOSÉ DA SILVA XAVIER (1748–1792) Born near São João del Rei and nicknamed Tiradentes, or the Toothpuller, he led a revolutionary movement inspired by the French Revolution in the late eighteenth century. He was captured and brutally executed but became a national hero and is recognized as the father of Brazilian independence.

NAIR DE TEFFE (1887–1945) The wife of President Hermes da Fonseca (1910–1914), she was known for her defiance of upper-class manners by smoking, frequenting bars, and playing the guitar. She also worked as a newspaper caricaturist and became a patron of musical and theatrical groups.

GETULIO VARGAS (1883–1954) President of Brazil from 1930 to 1945, and again from 1951 until 1954, Vargas was born in São Borja. His sweeping reforms of Brazil's economy and society were accompanied by censorship, harsh repression, and one-party rule.

THE FERNANDO DE NORONHA ARCHIPELAGO The archipelago is a protected island chain lying off the coast of Pernambuco state. The unique ecosystem of this area attracts tourists and scientists from all over the world.

IGUAÇU FALLS On the border of Brazil, Argentina, and Paraguay, 275 separate waterfalls surge down a 3-mile (4.8-km) stretch of the Paraná River.

ITAIPÚ DAM Completed in 1991 by Paraquay and Brazil, the Itaipú Dam's eighteen generating units can produce up to 12,600 megawatts of electricity. The dam supplies about 25 percent of Brazil's energy and about 78 percent of Paraguay's.

JOAQUINA BEACH Brazil's best-known surfing beach is in the state of Santa Catarina. The national surfing championships are held here each year.

MARACANA STADIUM Located in Rio de Janeiro, this soccer stadium is the largest in the world. It can pack in more than 150,000 spectators.

MUSEUM OF CONTEMPORARY ART Located in Niterói, the Museum of Contemporary Art displays twentieth-century and contemporary art. The collection includes works by Picasso, Chagall, Matisse, and many others, including the greatest contemporary Brazilian artists.

PANTANAL A vast wilderness of rivers, streams, and wetlands in Mato Grosso, south central Brazil, the Pantanal hosts the most diverse freshwater ecosystem in the world.

SAMBÓDROMO Also known as the Sambadrome, this "dance stadium" of grandstand-lined streets in Rio de Janeiro is where competing samba schools hold Carnaval parades each February.

SÃO MIGUEL DAS MISSOES View the ruins of a Jesuit mission in Rio Grande do Sul, Brazil's southernmost state.

SERRA DA CAPIVARA NATIONAL PARK This park in the state of Piauí contains ancient rock paintings, some of which are at least 25,000 years old.

SUGARLOAF MOUNTAIN This peak in Rio de Janeiro towers over the city, nearby hills, and a winding coastline. A cable car reaches the top of the mountain every thirty minutes.

TEATRO AMAZONAS An opera house completed in 1896, during the rubber boom, the Teatro Amazonas in Manaus was designed in an imitation of Italian Rennaisance style by an architectural firm in Lisbon, Portugal.

animism: the belief that inanimate objects and forces of nature have conscious life

bandeirantes: explorers who settled western Brazil and Amazonia beginning in the eighteenth century

bossa nova: popular music of Brazilian origin, related to the samba but with complex jazzlike qualities

candomblé: an Afro-Brazilian religion of Yoruba origin developed by African slaves from Nigeria and their descendants. Practitioners of candomblé were often forced to outwardly equate their deities with Catholic saints in order to avoid persecution.

capoeira: a martial art in which opponents use a variety of dancelike moves as well as simple weapons

captaincy: one of fifteen territories constituted in colonial Brazil, each under the direct rule of a governor designated by the king

cariocas: the nickname for residents of Rio de Janeiro

Carnaval: the annual pre-Lenten festival, which started in Rio de Janeiro in 1840

cerrado: the subtropical forest that dominates the landscape of Brazil's Central Plateau

choro: a musical style beginning in the nineteenth century, in which street musicians of Rio de Janeiro lent their particular style to European songs and dances

cortiços: urban apartment blocks, often home to working-class and poor Brazilians

degredados: political exiles or prisoners who were banished to Brazil when it was a colony of Portugal

episcopate: a religious seat, or place from where priests exercise authority

favelas: urban shantytowns, often built by poor refugees from rural areas of Brazil

feijoada: a popular stew originating in meals prepared by Brazilian slaves. Sometimes called Brazil's national dish, feijoada is commonly made up of roast pork, beans, and rice.

garimpeiros: amateur gold miners who have wrought environmental destruction as well as violence among the indigenous peoples of northern Brazil

gauchos: ranchers and cowboys of the plains of southern Brazil

jeito: the ability to solve a problem by bending the rules and regulations, a talent widely admired in Brazil

mamelucos: a term for people descended from mixed European and indigenous ancestors. Also known as caboclos.

manganese: a metallic element that resembles iron but is not magnetic

manioc: a root plant native to Brazil that is eaten like potatoes or used to make flour

maracá: a musical instrument made from a gourd filled with pebbles or seeds

Mercosul: an association of several South American countries that works to increase trade among these countries

paulistas: the nickname for residents of São Paulo

quilombo: a town or region settled and cultivated by escaped slaves

samba: a dance originally brought to Brazil by African slaves and that developed into a national craze in the 1920s

sertão: the dry backlands of the northeast, subject to frequent drought

sesmarias: estates granted by captaincy governors to Brazil's colonial settlers

telenovelas: prime-time television soap operas that have captured a huge audience in Brazil

umbanda: a spirit-possession religion that emerged in Brazil in the 1920s. The religion combines cultural elements from Africa, Europe, and pre-colonial Brazil.

Yoruba: a language of southwestern Nigeria and parts of Benin and Togo; also, a member of any of the Yoruba-speaking peoples

Brazil. Alexandria, VA: Time-Life Books, 1988.
An anecdotal introduction to Brazil for the armchair traveler.

Fausto, Boris. *A Concise History of Brazil.* Cambridge, UK:
Cambridge University Press, 1999.
A useful, academic description of Brazilian history, from the Portuguese colonization to the 1990s.

Görgen, Hermann M. *Brazil: Impressions and Insight.* Innsbruck,
Austria: Pinguin-Verlag, 1998.
An evocative photo album of modern Brazil.

"PRB 2001 World Population Data Sheet." *Population Reference
Bureau (PRB).* 2002.
Website: <http://www.prb.org> (October 5, 2001).
Annual statistics sheet that provides a wealth of population, demographic, and health statistics for Brazil and almost all countries in the world.

Richard, Christopher. *Brazil.* New York: Marshall Cavendish, 1999.
A well-illustrated school/library volume giving general information on Brazil's geography, history, and culture.

Rocha, Jan. *Brazil: A Guide to the People, Politics, and Culture.*
New York: Interlink Books, 1999.
An in-depth travel guide, including chapters on politics, economics, history, and culture and covering issues affecting modern Brazilians.

Skidmore, Thomas E. *Brazil: Five Centuries of Change.* New York:
Oxford University Press, 1999.
A scholarly history of Brazil, beginning in 1500 and covering political, economic, and social issues through the date of publication.

U.S. Department of State Bureau of European Affairs. *Country
Profiles.* April, 2001.
Website: <http://www.state.gov/r/pa/ei/bgn/> (October 9, 2001).
Profiles of countries, including Brazil, produced by the U.S. Department of State. Profiles include brief summaries of geography, people, government and politics, and economy.

Selected Bibliography

Amado, Jorge. *Dona Flor and Her Two Husbands.* **New York: Dimensions, 1998.**
A funny and entertaining novel about a young woman in Bahia who is haunted by the ghost of her husband.

Ben-Vindo Ao Brasil (Welcome to Brazil).
Website: <http://www.uoregon.edu/~sergiok/brasil.html>
A virtual tour of Brazil, with statistics, history, environment, social issues, weather, news, economic and financial information, health issues, phone listings, and useful links.

The Brazilian Embassy in Washington.
Website: <http://www.brasilemb.org/>
This official site offers the Brazilian government's outlook on U.S. and international events, policy statements on global warming and deforestation, information on travel to Brazil, and much more.

CIA World Factbook: Brazil.
Website: <http://www.cia.gov/cia/publications/factbook/geos/br.html>
Useful facts, statistics, political and economic information, and background information on Brazil.

Hecht, Tobias. *At Home in the Street: Street Children of Northeast Brazil.* **Cambridge, UK: Cambridge University Press, 1998.**
An analytical study and description of street children in modern Brazil, set in the form of stories told and questions asked by the subjects themselves.

Herndon, William Lewis, Gary Kinder, and Lardner Gibbon.
Exploration of the Valley of the Amazon. **New York: Grove Press, 2000.**
The story of Captain William Lewis Herndon, who traveled the length of the Amazon valley by foot, canoe, and mule train in 1851–1852.

Hilton, Christopher S. *Ayrton Senna: As Time Goes By.* **Newbury Park, CA: Haynes Publications, Inc., 1999.**
Story of the late driver Ayrton Senna, describing his life in and out of racing in Brazil and England and his experiences as a top Formula One driver.

Levine, Robert M. *The Brazil Reader: History, Culture, Politics.* **Raleigh, NC: Duke University Press, 1999.**
More than one hundred short essays describing daily life and work in Brazil.

Maria Brazil.
Website: <http://www.maria-brazil.org/>
Advertised as the "Home of Brazilian Culture on the Web," this lively personal site offers information about Brazilian art, music, food, folklore, and related books.

McGowan, Chris. *The Brazilian Sound: Samba, Bossa Nova, and the Popular Music of Brazil.* **Philadelphia, PA: Temple University Press, 1998.**
A guide to Brazilian popular music, including informative interviews with Antônio Carlos Jobim, Milton Nascimento, and many others.

Further Reading and Websites

Parnell, Helga. *Cooking the South American Way.* **Minneapolis, MN: Lerner Publications Company, 2003.**
A number of recipes from Brazil appear in this collection of recipes from South America.

Roosevelt, Theodore. *Through the Brazilian Wilderness.* **Lanham, MD: Cooper Square Press, 2000.**
A firsthand account of Theodore Roosevelt's 1914 journey down the "River of Doubt," an Amazon tributary (now the Rio Roosevelt), on a mapping expedition for the American Museum of Natural History.

Schepre-Hughes, Nancy. *Death without Weeping: The Violence of Everyday Life in Brazil.* **Berkeley: University of California Press, 1993.**
A description of life in a shantytown in northern Brazil and the sickness and starvation dealt with by poor Brazilian families.

Schlener, Paul L. *Port of Two Brothers.* **Harrisburg, PA: ABWE Publishing, 2000.**
Account of day-to-day life and struggles of missionaries working among the Ticuna people of the Amazon region.

Teissl, Helmut. *Carnival in Rio.* **New York: Abbeville Press, 2000.**
A photo essay on the festival of Carnaval, including a CD of Carnaval music.

Updike, John. *Brazil.* **New York: Alfred A. Knopf, 1994.**
A novel that sets the old Germanic legend of Tristan and Isolde in modern Rio de Janeiro.

vgsbooks.com
Website: <http://www.vgsbooks.com>
Visit vgsbooks.com, the homepage of the Visual Geography Series®. You can get linked to all sorts of useful on-line information, including geographical, historical, demographic, cultural, and economic websites. The vgsbooks.com site is a great resource for late-breaking news and statistics.

Captions for photos appearing on the cover and chapter openers:

Cover: Sugarloaf Mountain and Rio de Janeiro glow at night.

pp. 4–5 The urban skyline of Pôrto Alegre shimmers along Brazil's east coast.

pp. 8–9 The Iguaçu Falls is a series of hundreds of waterfalls along a 3-mile (4.8-km) stretch of the Paraná River.

pp. 22–23 This prehistoric rock painting near Januária, Brazil, was created sometime between 7500 and 4000 B.C.

pp. 38–39 Women and children attend church in the state of Bahia.

pp. 44–45 Samba school dancers enjoy participating in a Carnaval parade in Rio de Janeiro.

pp. 56–57 The Itaipú Dam on Brazil's border with Paraguay has the capacity to produce enough electricity to meet the power needs of a state as populous as California.

Photo Acknowledgments
The images in this book are reproduced with the permission of: © SuperStock, pp. 4–5, 12, 13, 14, 20, 21; PresentationMaps.com, pp. 6, 18; VARIG Airlines, pp. 8–9; © TRIP/J. Sweeney, p. 10; © TRIP/M. Keep, p. 11; © Wolfgang Kaehler, pp. 15, 68; © Stephanie Maze/CORBIS, pp. 17, 38–39, 44–45, 51, 59; © TRIP/ P. Musson, p. 19; © Pierre Colombel/CORBIS, pp. 22–23; © Independent Picture Service, pp. 24–25; © Ecoscene/CORBIS, p. 27; © Eye Ubiquitous/CORBIS, p. 29; © Musée du Louvre, Paris/SuperStock, p. 30; © Bettmann/CORBIS, pp. 32, 34, 46; © AP/Wide World Photo, p. 35; © AFP/CORBIS, pp. 37, 42, 65; © TRIP/ASK IMAGES, p. 40; © Inge Yspeert/CORBIS, p. 47; © Reuters NewMedia Inc./CORBIS, pp. 49, 63; New York Cosmos, p. 53; © TRIP/M. Barlow, pp. 56–57; © TRIP/TWINK CARTER, p. 61; © Beth Davidow/Visuals Unlimited, p. 64; Laura Westlund, p. 69.

Cover photo: © SuperStock. Back cover photo: NASA.